OPENING
THE
CLERGY
PARACHUTE

OPENING THE CLERGY PARACHUTE

SOFT LANDINGS FOR CHURCH LEADERS WHO ARE SEEKING A CHANGE

CHRISTOPHER C. MOORE

Abingdon Press
Nashville

OPENING THE CLERGY PARACHUTE:
SOFT LANDINGS FOR CHURCH LEADERS WHO ARE SEEKING A CHANGE

This book is printed on recycled, acid-free paper.

Library of Congress Cataloging-in-Publication Data

Moore, Christopher Chamberlin.
    Opening the clergy parachute: soft landings for church leaders seeking a change/Christopher Chamberlin Moore.
        p.   cm.
    Includes bibliographical references and index.
    ISBN 0-687-08659-0 (pbk : alk. paper)
        1. Clergy—United States—Relocation.   2. Clergy—United States—Secular employment.   I. Title.
BV664.M66   1995   94-24117
253'.2—dc20

Most Scripture quotations are from the New Revised Standard Version Bible, Copyright 1989 by the Division of Christian Education of the National Council of the Churches of Christ in the USA. Used by permission.

Those noted RSV are from the Revised Standard Version of the Bible, copyright 1946, 1952, 1971 by the Division of Christian Education of the National Council of Churches of Christ in the USA. Used by permission.

The After-Interview Checklist on pp. 99-100 is adapted from the *Job Counselor's Manual* by Nathan Afrin and Victoria A. Basalel, published by University Park Press in 1980.

"The Cost of a Professional Ministry" on pp. 104-105 is adapted from *How to Pay Your Pastor More and Balance the Budget Too* by Manfred Holck, Jr., published by Church Management, Inc., in 1988 and reissued by Logos Publications, Invergrove, Minn.

95 96 97 98 99 00 01 02 03 04 05—10 9 8 7 6 5 4 3 2 1

MANUFACTURED IN THE UNITED STATES OF AMERICA

To
Janice,
Alice, *and* Douglas,
beloved companions
on my journey
And in memory
of my father,
John F. C. Moore,
who first awakened in me
an interest in understanding
the meaning of
a person's work

ACKNOWLEDGMENTS

I would like to thank the many gifted and dedicated clergy who have shared their lives and ministries with me in the course of my research and writing for this book. They demonstrated, through their struggles, the need for such a book, and were themselves the source of many insightful observations about the clergy selection process.

I also would like to thank the following clergy and denominational representatives for supplying me with information on the clergy placement practices of the major denominations: The Reverend Earl R. Jefferson, Director of Christian Education, African Methodist Episcopal Church; the Right Reverend Cecil Bishop, Presiding Bishop of the Third Episcopal District, African Methodist Episcopal Zion Church; the Reverend Jean A. Feiler, Director of Enrollment, American Baptist Personnel Services, American Baptist Church; the Reverend Dr. George O. Wood, General Secretary, and the Reverend Dr. Joseph R. Flower, retired General Secretary, Assemblies of God; the Reverend Joyce B. Coalson, Vice President, Center for Leadership and Ministry, and Ms. Joyce Beloat, Executive, Department of Ministry, Division of Homeland Ministries, Christian Church (Disciples of Christ); the Reverend Larry G. Hess, Director, Office of Ministerial Development, Church of God (Cleveland, Tennessee); the Reverend Jack Stone, General Secretary, Church of the Nazarene; the Reverend Bruce Wadzeck, Princeton Church of Christ, Churches of Christ; the Reverend James G. Wilson, Executive Director, Church Deployment Office, The Episcopal Church; the Reverend Lowell G. Almen, Secretary, and the Reverend Dr. Thomas Blevins, Director, Department of Synodal Relations, Evangelical Lutheran Church in America; the Reverend Dr. William F. Meyer, Executive Director, Board for Higher Education, and the Reverend David G. Schmiel, former Executive Director, The Lutheran Church-Missouri Synod; Mr. Ross Cook, Business Administrator, Presbyterian Church in America; the Reverend R. Howard McCuen, Jr., Associate for Services to Committees on Ministry, Mrs. Evelyn Hwang, Coordinator of Personnel Referral Services, and Ms. Agnes Holswade, Associate for Operations, Presbyterian Church (USA); the Reverend Alvin J. Poppen, Coordinator of Human Resources, Reformed Church in America; Pastor Martin Webber, Associate Editor, *Ministry*, Seventh-day Adventist Church; Dr. Mark

ACKNOWLEDGMENTS

Coppenger, Vice President for Convention Relations, Executive Committee, Ms. Joan A. Redford, Administrative Assistant to the President, and the Reverend Dr. Ray Pollard, Baptist General Association of Virginia, Southern Baptist Convention; the Reverend Daniel D. Hotchkiss, Ministerial Settlement Director, Unitarian Universalist Association; the Reverend Charlotte Still, Minister for Placement, and Ms. Stephanie H. Nelson, Placement Coordinator, Office for Church Life and Leadership, United Church of Christ; and the Reverend Richard Yeager, Director of Evaluation and Continuing Education, The United Methodist Church.

I thank also the Right Reverend G. P. Mellick Belshaw, retired Bishop of the Episcopal Diocese of New Jersey, who gave me the opportunity to turn my interest in clergy placement into a professional work; the Reverend Roy Lewis, director of the Northeast Career Center, who generously shared insights about clergy career transitions; the Reverend James G. Wilson, executive director of the Church Deployment Office in New York, and my colleagues in the Vacancy Sharing Consultation, in whose always enjoyable company I learned how the system works; my editor, Dr. Paul Franklyn, a source of wise counsel and insightful advice; and my secretary, Denise Bushnell, who completed the final manuscript of *Opening the Clergy Parachute* by the deadline, in spite of an undiagnosed fracture from a fall three days before. For these and others too numerous to name, I am deeply grateful.

Finally, I would like to acknowledge all clergy who struggle courageously to understand how God would have them serve, and how their particular gifts, abilities, and sense of call translate into the requirements of a ministry in the church or in some alternative path. It is for such individuals that this book is written.

Christopher Chamberlin Moore
Ewing, New Jersey

CONTENTS

CONTENTS

PART TWO: Exploring New Possibilities

Two cardinal rules for successful placement. Resources: denominational staff; positions-open listings; personal networks; computer matching; vacancy-sharing consultations; local and regional listings; seminary offices; classified ads; job fairs; resources for women and minorities; specialized positions; missions; opportunities abroad. The three deployment methods of the major denominations. Formal and informal channels. Your first contact with a church. Personal visits to the area. Practical guidelines during your search.

Sources of information: the church itself; denominational office; your network; other sources. Areas of concern: financial data; membership and attendance figures; socioeconomic characteristics; previous leadership; church "personality"; stated goals of the congregation; staff; power structure. Weighing a call or placement. Dealing with the "Halo Effect." How much to compromise.

Identifying what the church is looking for. The one big question on their minds. Preparing for your interview. Six rules for successful candidating. Typical questions and ways to respond. Questions for you to ask. The role of the clergy spouse in the interview. Dealing with the tough or dysfunctional committee. The issue of clergy privacy. Interviewing for a staff position. Follow-up. First steps if the church extends a call or a placement is made.

Why you need a Letter of Agreement. Identifying what you want in advance. The secret of win-win negotiating. Supplemental clergy benefits and costs of doing ministry. Housing issues. Negotiating your cash salary: arguments to use; arguments *not* to use. The clergy performance review.

Chapter 9: Endings and Beginnings / 117

Dealing with "Buyer's Remorse." Terminating with your present church. Personal and family stress. Buying and selling a house. Safeguarding your possessions and your sanity during the move. The first few days. What the "honeymoon" *really* is. Women's start-up issues. Planning your institution. Initiating change—when and how to do it. Beginning to shape a new ministry.

PART THREE: Special Circumstances

Chapter 10: Creative Solutions for Women, Minorities, and 55-and-Over Clergy / 129

Ten placement strategies that work. Particular strategies for: female clergy; racial and ethnic minorities; clergy 55 and older; singles and/or divorced; clergy couples; terminated, problem-plagued, or short-tenured clergy; reentry clergy; "downsizing" clergy. Turning your handicap into an asset.

Chapter 11: Career Alternatives for Those Who Want Out / 140

Analyzing what you hope to gain in secular employment. Identifying opportunities in the secular workplace. Easing the transition.

Chapter 12: Epilogue—Abram and Sarai: A Model for Clergy Transition / 149

Appendix A: Methods of Clergy Placement in Selected Major Denominations / 151

African Methodist Episcopal Church; African Methodist Episcopal Zion Church; American Baptist Churches in the U.S.A.; Assemblies

CONTENTS

of God; Christian Church (Disciples of Christ); Church of God (Cleveland, Tenn.); Church of the Nazarene; Churches of Christ; The Episcopal Church; Evangelical Lutheran Church in America; The Lutheran Church—Missouri Synod; Presbyterian Church in America; Presbyterian Church (U.S.A.); Reformed Church in America; Seventh-day Adventist Church; Southern Baptist Convention; Unitarian Universalist Association; United Church of Christ; The United Methodist Church.

PART ONE: Getting Ready for a Move

Chapter One

CLERGY PLACEMENT
Making the System Work for You

The LORD said to Abram, "Go from your country and your kindred and your father's house to the land that I will show you. I will make of you a great nation . . . so that you will be a blessing."

Genesis 12:1-2

Moving on. Taking leave. Saying good-bye to all that is old and familiar. Preparing to face new challenges. And all in order to be a greater blessing to others. Encountering transition is one of the hallmarks of the modern ordained ministry.

Dave Rogers[1] has been pastor of a mid-sized suburban church for eleven years. Dave has had a fulfilling ministry. The congregation likes him, and Dave feels comfortable in this church. But sometimes he feels *too* comfortable. Dave is forty-eight, and he wonders whether he should make one more move before retirement—perhaps to a larger congregation.

Jane Murphy is an assistant at a large, multistaff church. Two years out of seminary, she is looking forward to having her own church. But, as a woman in ministry, she wonders whether she will be called to be senior pastor as easily as she entered a staff position directly out of seminary.

Earl Smith is an African American pastor of a historically black congregation in the inner city. Earl would like to be considered for a broader range of opportunities in the church. He wonders whether he could serve as pastor of a multiracial, or even a predominantly white congregation.

Dave, Jane, and Earl are part of an estimated fifty thousand clergy—one in five currently serving in congregational ministry—who move each year. At any given time, an equal number of clergy probably are considering seeking a new call or a new placement. And all are wrestling with certain basic questions: How do I know when it is time to move? How can I present myself as an attractive candidate for new positions in the church? Above all—will I actually be called to a new position, and if so, how will I know whether this is the right position for me?

I am a clergy placement officer in one of the major denominations.[2] I work on a daily basis with ministers like Dave, Jane, and Earl, who are considering relocating. I also work with congregations that are looking for a new pastor. In the course of my work, I have come to know the considerations that lie behind a congregation's decision to call a new minister, and also the factors that clergy need to take into account in seeking a new call. In this book, I discuss *when* to leave your present position, *where* to go, and *what* to do when you get there. This book is a comprehensive guide for clergy of all the major denominations who are actively seeking a new call.

A NEW BALANCE OF POWER

Clergy do not need to be told that in recent years, the balance of power in the church has shifted away from ordained clergy and toward the lay members of the church. Nowhere is this more evident than in the placement process. Lay people have a greater voice than ever before in deciding who will be their pastor. Clergy seeking a new position often find themselves at a disadvantage in dealing with this reality. It often seems that search committees are provided full and complete information about how the process works, while clergy struggle on with few resources provided for them. Furthermore, members of a search committee enjoy strength in numbers, while clergy typically negotiate the process alone, perhaps with minimal assistance provided by a denominational staff person, along with the emotional support of a spouse.

One purpose for this book is to help redress the balance of power between clergy and lay people in the placement process, and to provide the "tools" clergy need to negotiate the process more effectively.

Opportunities Are Opening Up

The employment logjam that has existed for clergy for the better part of the past two decades is beginning to break up. An estimated one-third of clergy in many mainstream denominations will retire during the next decade. An increasing number of positions are expected to become available during the coming decade in all the major denominations.

"It's a great time to be an able person in ministry," remarked one American Baptist Church executive recently.

It *is* a great time—*if* you avoid a couple of pitfalls that clergy typically encounter as they prepare to begin a search for a new position.

The Medical Model and the Cinderella Complex

Many clergy contemplating a change in their ministry defeat themselves before they begin, by succumbing to either the Medical Model or the Cinderella Complex. The Medical Model assumes that in a job search, there is no need to define one's ministry adequately, because there exists somewhere "out there" a Wise Person (perhaps one's bishop or a search committee head) who will recognize our true abilities, "diagnose" where we should serve, and automatically slot us into the right position.

Related to the Medical Model is the Cinderella Complex, which looks for a Handsome Prince (or Princess)—again in the form of a search committee head—who will rescue us from drudgery in our small congregation and invite us to live forever in the Castle in the Clouds (one of the major churches of the denomination). Needless to say, neither the Medical Model nor the Cinderella Complex is an adequate paradigm for the reality of the competitive clergy job market. Today, clergy must "diagnose" themselves (i.e., adequately define their own ministry, perhaps with the assistance of a denominational placement officer and/or one of the clergy career development centers), and must serve as their own Handsome Prince (or Princess) in getting from where they are to where they want to be.

The problem with both the Medical Model and the Cinderella Complex is that they imply that clergy themselves have little or no direct control over what happens in the placement process. Both result from a common assumption among clergy that 80 percent of success in placement is the result of factors "out there" (i.e., the number of positions available at any given moment), and/or the result of factors over which clergy have no direct control (age and gender, for example); and perhaps 20 percent is the result of factors over which clergy do have control (the effectiveness of their search). As a placement officer, it has been my observation that, in most circumstances, the ratios are exactly reversed. Eighty percent of success is the result of factors over which clergy *do* have control—how disciplined they are in their search, how well they present themselves—and perhaps only 20 percent is the result of factors "out there." As Richard Nelson Bolles, the author of the best-selling job-hunting guide, *What Color Is Your Parachute?* has written, "By and large the major difference between successful and unsuccessful job-hunters is *the way they go about their job hunt*—not some factors 'out there.'"[3]

Seeing God's Hand in the Process

One question is often asked in connection with the placement process: Has the whole concept of *call* been lost in the *process?* This is an important question, because if clergy cannot see how the theology of call correlates with the placement process, the most likely outcome is that they will adopt a passive stance and lose their effectiveness as candidates, or even as pastors after they are placed.

In relating the theology of call to placement, it may be helpful to realize that the search process is, in reality, two separate but interrelated processes. The first is one of prayerful discernment. The model is the prophet Elijah in First Kings 19, who sits on the mountaintop, waiting for guidance from Yahweh, which comes finally in the form of a "still small voice." The second part of the process is one of directed action. The model is still Elijah, but now he is commissioned by Yahweh to accomplish particular tasks in the world. The two parts of the process—prayerful discernment, followed by direct action—are separate but interrelated. After all, it takes directed action early in the process for Elijah to get to his mountaintop, as it also takes directed action on our part for us to engage in an intensive process of ministry review before starting our search. And it takes discernment during the second part of the process, for Elijah to perceive the way he is to carry out the Lord's commandments, as it also takes discernment on our part to determine whether a particular church is indeed the place where the Lord wants us to be.

16

One Inescapable Factor

It would be misleading to write this chapter without emphasizing that the one inescapable factor in successful placement is a proven record of competence in one's present position. This is the quality that I, as a placement officer, look for in prospective candidates for churches in my own denomination. This is the quality that churches are increasingly expecting. They want candidates who have *made a difference* in their present church—and who can point to exactly what that difference is. Without a record of competence, all the rest—placement materials, interviewing, and so on—is simply window dressing.

So important is this quality of competence that denominational leaders advise candidates who are experiencing a slump in their present ministry to put their job seeking on hold for a year or two, if at all possible, while they reactivate their present ministry, then resume their search when they have some real achievements to point to.

OVERVIEW OF THE PROCESS

Moving from one church to another—or to another ministry entirely—is a long and complex process. Some specific aspects of that process are discussed in this book:

Deciding When to Go

Some clergy stay too long in their present position. Others move prematurely or for the wrong reasons. I explain factors to consider in deciding when to move (chapter 2).

Defining Your Ministry

The first step in placement is to become clear in your own mind as to exactly what it is you are seeking in your new call. I explain how to define gifts and abilities, personal goals and objectives (chapter 3).

Preparing Materials

Your placement materials must accurately reflect the person you are and the ministry you offer. I explain how to prepare your Pastor's Profile, résumé, and other written materials (chapter 4).

Identifying Vacancies

The wise candidate chooses from a wide variety of ministry opportunities. I discuss some obvious and less obvious ways of discovering potential vacancies (chapter 5).

Casing a Church

You want not just a church—you want the *right* church. I discuss some factors to be considered in making the right match (chapter 6).

Candidating and Interviewing

The one-on-one contact between you and a prospective church is the most crucial single item in the candidating process. I explain techniques for effective interviewing, questions to be asked of a prospective church, and how to use candidating week as a data-gathering, as well as a self-marketing opportunity (chapter 7).

Negotiating a Letter of Agreement

Negotiating a salary and benefits package you can live with is an item of utmost importance for clergy and their families. I explain the major elements of such a package (chapter 8).

That Crucial First Year

The first year is make-or-break time for a new ministry. I discuss some do's and don'ts of the start-up (chapter 9).

Special Deployment Concerns

Female clergy, minority candidates, and age-55-and-over clergy have special concerns and issues in connection with the placement process. I explain placement strategies for these and other candidates (chapter 10).

Alternative Career Options

For perfectly good reasons, some clergy decide to leave the professional ministry, either temporarily or for good. I explain alternative career opportunities for clergy in the secular world (chapter 11).

In addition to the topics and information above, the appendix of this book lists a wealth of up-to-date information for clergy in transition, including a checklist of job-search tasks, a list of the names and addresses of church career development centers across the country, and a complete bibliography. Also included is a summary of placement procedures used in nineteen of the major denominations. Clergy reading this book can refer to the appendix for specific details about how the process works, including printed and other resources available from their particular denominations.

Language and Terminology

Recognizing that members of the ordained ministry are female as well as male in most of the major denominations, I have chosen to use *they* when referring to individual clergy throughout this book. This avoids the awkward repetition of "he or she," and also reflects the fact that, in most cases, I am referring to clergy as a group, even though a single member of that group is used in a particular example.

Placement terminology varies from one denomination to another. In some denominations, clergy are called pastors; in others, priests or ministers. Clergy placement is called variously clergy deployment, settlement, appointment, or relocation. Judicatory heads are called variously bishops, district superintendents, elders, presbyters, executives, pastors, and so forth. In order to maintain consistency throughout the book, I usually refer to members of the ordained ministry as *pastors* or *ministers;* to the clergy selection process as *clergy placement;* to the ministerial selection committee as the *search committee;* and to the local denominational superior as the *judicatory head.* If this is not exactly what these are called in your denomination, please know that I *am* talking about you and your denomination as well. In the appendix of this book, where placement procedures of the major denominations are summarized, the terminology appropriate to each of the particular denominations is used.

Gifts and Placement

As a member of the ordained ministry, God has given you real gifts. It is important for you, for your family, for your congregations—past, present, and future—and ultimately for God, that your gifts be expressed where they may bear the most fruit.

As a placement officer, I firmly believe that there is no reason for clergy to remain "stuck" in an unproductive ministry. There are real opportunities awaiting able and energetic pastors who seek a new call, and there will be more and more such opportunities in the years ahead. All that is needed in order to respond to these opportunities is for you to exercise initiative and commitment, working within the placement guidelines of your particular denomination.

The purpose of this book is to assist you in taking this exciting and challenging next step in your ministry.

Chapter Two

WHEN TO SEEK A NEW BEGINNING

The wise mind will know the time and way.

Ecclesiastes 8:5*b*

When to seek a new call or appointment is one of the toughest decisions you will face throughout your ministry. On the one hand, you feel loyalty and love toward the people you presently serve. On the other hand, you sense pressing personal and career issues that would argue in favor of a move. And to complicate the matter, you probably feel some guilt over the fact that personal considerations are playing a part in your decision. What, in fact, are valid reasons for seeking a new call?

VALID REASONS

The Church's Needs Have Changed

Over time, the needs of a particular church change. The needs that called you there in the first place may have been met, or may no longer exist. When you arrived at St. Swithin's five years ago, the church needed to get more involved in the community. You accomplished that, and now, five years later, St. Swithin's offers a variety of community outreach programs. What is needed now is a warm and loving pastor to carry on the ministry that you established—not another five years of a hard driver like yourself.

The fact is, church needs *do* change. Furthermore, our own understanding of our gifts and abilities tends to become more clear over time. In some cases, we realize that our abilities were never really well suited to the needs of our present church. If any of the above is true of you, it may be time to consider a change in your ministry.

Renewal of Ministry

While no pastor need necessarily "go stale" after serving the same church for a period of time, sometimes an actual physical move can put the spark back into ministry. A natural transition point occurs at some time between the seventh and eleventh years in a current ministry, and that may be an especially good time to make an intentional decision about whether to stay or move on. Some denominational environments seem to accelerate the time between transitions so that averages of two to four years are the norm. The stresses and cost to congregations and clergy of such rapid deployment are readily apparent.

Career Advancement

Career advancement is an uncomfortable concept for many clergy. We have been taught that the striving for "upward mobility," so common in business, is inappropriate for us. At the same time, clergy also experience the pull to respond to wider opportunities for service, and to enjoy the rewards that these opportunities bring. Put in the proper context, there is no reason career advancement should not be a valid reason for relocating. Jesus' commendation in Matthew 25:23 (RSV), "Well done, good and faithful servant; you have been faithful over a little, I will set you over much," certainly seems to suggest that God rewards faithful and effective service.

If you are considering a career-related move and feel somewhat ambivalent about your motives, ask yourself this: Is your desire to move primarily an appropriate desire to serve on a wider scale, or is it largely a desire for the "perks" of a larger ministry?

Still another consideration, in the context of career advancement, is your present age. The "golden years" for placement in a new ministry are 35 to 45. Opportunities begin to restrict after 50, and at 55, even a lateral move may be difficult.

Family Concerns

You do not live in a vacuum. Family considerations may involve valid reasons for seeking a new call or placement.

The salary that may have been sufficient for you when you were right out of seminary or starting on your career may no longer adequately support your family in its active years, plus allowing you to put money aside for your children's college education.

The nature of your present community is also a consideration. Is yours a community where you want your children to spend their formative years? What are the opportunities for cultural and educational growth, and for other amenities?

Another major factor is your spouse's employment opportunities. If your spouse is the primary breadwinner and has been offered greater opportunities out of the area, it may make sense for you to seek out ministry opportunities in the new area.

Finally, how does your family feel about the prospect of moving? Probably there is no "good" time for young children to be uprooted, but some times are better than others (i.e., when they change schools, for example). Is this time one of those?

Church Conflict

Is church conflict a reason for seeking a new call? The answer: It depends.

Factors to be considered are the level and extent of the conflict; whether or not it involves the core leadership of the congregation; the probable effects on the church of your leaving, on the one hand, or your staying to resolve the issues, on the other; and finally, your emotional ability and that of your family to deal with an extended period of conflict and unrest.

In general, leaving would tend to be indicated, *if:* the level and extent of the conflict is widespread; it involves the core leadership of the congregation in conflict with you, not just a fringe group within the church; the effect on the church would tend to be extremely damaging if you stayed; and finally, neither you nor your family possess the emotional resources to weather an extended period of conflict and unrest in the church.

Seeking an answer to issues such as these is not something you want to attempt alone, as both you and your family are highly emotionally involved in this situation. Seek out a denominational official or some trusted colleague in ministry, and explore with them the nature of the situation and your best response to it. And, if at all possible, do not—repeat—*do not* resign your present position until you have accepted a new call, no matter how strong the pressure to resign may be.

What Do You Hope to Achieve?

The more clear you are in your own mind about exactly what you hope to achieve in seeking a new call, the more likely you are to realize the goals you have set for yourself and your ministry.

Before beginning your search, ask yourself some basic questions concerning your goals and objectives: Are you looking for *larger* responsibilities? Are you looking for a church where you can change the actual *focus* of your ministry? Do you want a different type of *community* in which to raise your children? Do you want a bigger *salary?* Don't be afraid to identify exactly what it is you hope to achieve as a result of seeking a new call.

Weighing the Pros and Cons

Take a piece of paper. On the left side, list the frustrations of your present ministry. Be candid and specific. Now draw a line down the middle of the paper. In the right-hand column, across from each of your frustrations, list a positive quality that would be the opposite of the frustration you listed. For example, if you listed this in the left-hand column: "Unwillingness of the church to consider the possibility of outreach ministry," then in the right-hand column, you might list the following as a desired positive quality: "Commitment on the part of the church to respond to the needs of the community."

After you have listed all the positives and negatives, take a pair of scissors and cut each positive quality into a separate piece of paper. Place your pile of separated listings on a table and arrange them in order of their importance to you. (You could accomplish this by rearranging on a word-processor screen.) When you have completed this, you will have a capsule description of the style of ministry, along with some elements of a personal lifestyle, to which you feel yourself called. Now ask yourself a fundamental question: Could I possibly achieve these things I have listed right where I am, or would achieving them necessarily involve a move?

If you have completed the exercise above and realize that you probably *could* achieve your desired objectives in your present ministry, yet nevertheless find yourself highly resistant to the idea of remaining where you are, then you have discovered that your energy is simply no longer in your present ministry, and it probably is time to consider a change.

Ways of conducting a more detailed ministry assessment are discussed in the next chapter.

The Importance of Timing

As a general rule, the time to seek a new call is when things are going well in your present ministry—not when they have begun to fall apart.

Unfortunately, many clergy avoid thinking about seeking a new call until after they have lost momentum in their present ministry. The problem is that by this time, they have no recent successes to point to, and they may even be in a conflict situation with their church.

Seeking a new call is, in some ways, analogous to selling a house. When you get ready to sell, the first thing you do is get the house in order. You paint the trim, put on new shutters, clean up the yard, and install a new rug in the family room. Finally, when the house looks so good you wonder why you are even thinking about selling, you put it on the market. In a similar fashion, the best time for putting *yourself* "on the market" is when your present ministry is going so well that you feel you could happily stay on forever.

TIME MANAGEMENT

Once you have made the decision to seek a new call, it is important to move quickly. The reason is simple. While you are considering other ministry possibilities, you will have a tendency to withdraw emotionally from your present church. Therefore, it is important not to allow the search process to drag out over an extended period of time.

Clergy experience problems in managing their time in seeking a new call, because the rhythm of church life tends to make it very difficult to give regular amounts of time to placement concerns. There will be a lull in church activities, and you make great progress in preparing your placement materials. Then suddenly Christmas closes in, or the Every Member Canvass, or the annual fair, and suddenly six weeks have gone by, and you find that you are no further along in your search. How do you guard against procrastination and keep your search on track?

The best advice for clergy of most denominations is to *schedule a regular time every week* for seeking a new call. Thursday morning, from 10:00 A.M. to 12:00 noon, for example, is placement time, and nothing—repeat—*nothing* gets in the way of this. Obviously, in some denominations (see appendix, on United Methodist clergy, for example), where clergy deployment is regulated according to annual timelines, the clergy still will need to plan specific times, say in late winter, to pursue the issues of their deployment with appropriate leaders.

Another valuable technique for keeping your search on track is to follow what author Barbara Sher calls the Buddy System.[1] Following the Buddy System, you schedule a regular time once a week to meet with another person—a trusted colleague, or perhaps your spouse— for the purpose of working on mutual goals. You help that person achieve their goals; they help you achieve yours. Each time you meet, you report back what you have done during the past week to achieve *your* goal, which is to seek a new call, and you describe what you intend to accomplish during the coming week. Having another person to "report back to" on a regular basis is a tremendous aid in keeping your search on track over the period of weeks and months that the typical search takes.

HOW LONG SHOULD A SEARCH TAKE?

Whether you follow a short timeline or a longer timeline in seeking a new call will depend largely upon whether you are under pressure to leave, or your present ministry is going well, and you can give your search the time it really deserves.

A Short Process

Naturally, a short process is indicated if you have been terminated, or forced to resign, or are otherwise under severe pressure to leave quickly. What do you do?

First, don't panic. You need your wits about you. Immediately, make an appointment to talk to a denominational executive and explore your options. If resigning from your present church would seem advisable, work out the best settlement package you can, preferably with the help of the denominational representative. Early on, sit down with your spouse and explore short-term and long-term employment and financial options. Then turn to chapter 5 of this book and review all the possible channels for identifying vacancies in your denomination; or to chapter 10 for a discussion of placement strategies for clergy who have been terminated or have left under pressure.

If you have not yet resigned, but are under pressure to do so, defuse some of this pressure by telling your board that you are currently seeking a new position. If, after some months, you still have not received a new call or appointment, and the pressure is mounting, indicate to the board a tentative date by which you expect to have a new position. Above all, if possible, try to avoid resigning until you are offered a new position. A currently employed candidate is always more attractive than one who is out of a job.

A Longer Process

A longer timeline is for those who are secure in their present ministry and have the luxury of developing a fully integrated job search. A two-year process is ideal. The first year is spent in getting ready for the search. This is called "positioning" yourself. The second year is for the search itself. This is called "marketing" yourself.

FIRST YEAR: "POSITIONING" YOURSELF

Your major goals during the first year of the search are as follows:
• Achieve clarity about exactly what sort of ministry you will be seeking.

Visualize clearly, in your own mind, the type of church or other ministry to which you feel called. What *size* church do you want to serve? What would be its *style* of ministry? What would be the characteristics of its membership, and of the *community* in which it is located? To explore your sense of call as it relates to the type of church or other ministry you wish to seek, turn to the next chapter of this book, then make an appointment with your judicatory supervisor (such as a district superintendent), or with one of the clergy career development centers listed in appendix D.
• Based on the nature of the ministry you will be seeking, prepare all the necessary placement materials.

Depending upon your denomination, these may include a minister's information sheet, a résumé, a computerized minister's profile, and possibly other documents. We will be looking more closely at placement materials in chapter 4.

• Maintain strength in your present ministry.

When you are beginning to explore other options, you will have a tendency to disengage emotionally from your present ministry. In order to counter this, you need to give extra effort to keeping your present ministry strong—and remaining committed to it throughout the duration of your search.

• "Fine-tune" your present ministry to reflect your gifts as a candidate.

If you intend to present yourself as a "church-growth pastor," for example, look at your present ministry in terms of church-growth characteristics. Have you organized a well-coordinated greeters program at your church? A new-member incorporation program? An active evangelism committee? Now is the time to begin such projects, if your present church does not currently have them, so that when you offer yourself as a church-growth pastor—or as possessing some other ministry specialty—you have experience in your present ministry to back up such claims.

• Prepare yourself physically and emotionally.

Clergy who have been in their present position for a long time may have let their physical appearance slip. That potbelly may be endearing to (or at least grudgingly accepted by) your present congregation, but it may prove to be much less endearing to the members of a prospective search committee. This first year may be a good opportunity to start that long-deferred conditioning program—under a doctor's supervision, of course.

To summarize, during this first year, you have:

■ Achieved clarity, in your own mind, about the type of ministry you are seeking.

■ Prepared placement materials appropriate to the position you are seeking.

■ Maintained a sense of strength and commitment in your present ministry.

■ Fine-tuned your present ministry to reflect the gifts you claim as a candidate.

■ Prepared yourself physically, emotionally, and spiritually for the search ahead.

Second Year: "Marketing" Yourself

During the second, active year of your search, you will follow the procedures mandated by your particular denomination to accomplish the following objectives:

Initiate contact with prospective churches.

Identify vacancies and make an initial contact by letter or phone. (In closed appointment systems, this kind of contact is strongly discouraged, though very large churches tend to initiate contact anyway. In such systems, the first year of "positioning" may be all that an individual can do to influence the guidance provided by bishops and superintendents.)

Follow through on your contacts.

Respond to interested churches (or executive pastors), corresponding promptly and sending whatever materials they require.

Candidate for available positions.

Host visiting search committees at your home church. Accept invitations to candidate at a prospective church.

Accept a new call.

After prayerful consideration and following a full mutual ministry exploration, accept a call to begin a ministry at a new church.

For a complete checklist of all major tasks to be accomplished during the search process, turn to appendix B.

The Single Most Important Ingredient

Probably the single most important element in any search is being clear in your mind about the nature of the ministry you are seeking. Whether you are in wide-open or closed appointive systems, knowing what you are looking for is the *necessary first step*, both in preparing effective placement materials and, later, in presenting yourself as a candidate. In the next chapter, we will discuss ways of defining the ministry you offer as we discuss "Your Ministry in 25 Words or Less."

Chapter Three

YOUR MINISTRY, IN TWENTY-FIVE WORDS OR LESS

What are you seeking?

Genesis 37:15*b*

Being clear in your own mind as to exactly what you are seeking in a new position is probably the single most important element in the entire placement process. All the other parts of the process—preparing your placement materials, deciding what possibilities to pursue, presenting yourself as a candidate—depend for their effectiveness upon your clarity regarding what you are seeking.

In this chapter, we will be looking at two basic questions regarding placement:

• What is the nature of your call as you perceive it, now and in the future?

• Where could your call be best expressed?

DEFINING YOUR MINISTRY

What is the nature of your call? Simply to say, "My call is to be the minister in charge of a congregation," or to say, "My call is to be in charge of the largest congregation that will accept me," is not an adequate description of call. In fact, nearly all of us have a *call within the call.* That is, we have particular activities we do unusually well—and experience great joy in doing—*within* the larger context of being the pastor of a church or of performing another specialized ministry. Furthermore, we encounter biblical precedent for this. The apostle Paul, for example, saw himself as "an apostle to the Gentiles" (Romans 11:13*b*). That was his *specific* call—not just to be an apostle of Christ, but to be an apostle to a particular group of people—the *Gentiles.*

In a similar fashion, *you* may feel yourself called to minister to particular kinds of people, or to express particular *gifts* for ministry. Some feel a call to a specialized ministry in the church or other institution. Still others feel a call to a ministry in the secular workplace.

The question is, What is the nature of *your* call as you currently understand it, and what would seem to be the best setting for its expression?

Resources for Discernment

In seeking to answer the question, "What is my call?" you may draw upon a variety of valuable resources. One is the network of clergy career development centers located throughout the country, and listed in appendix D of this book. Another is your denominational placement officer, or a superintendent, who may be able to give you valuable insights into the strengths of your ministry. Trusted colleagues and friends, including your spouse, may give helpful insights, as long as you allow for a possible subjective bias. Several recently published books may prove helpful in assisting you to sharpen and define your sense of call.[1] Finally, the chief resource, of course, is prayer, as a continuing source of strength, as well as to provide guidance throughout the entire search process.

FOOLING THE LEFT BRAIN

The following exercises are for those who would like to explore the nature of their call on their own.[2] They are intended to accomplish what career development expert Richard Nelson Bolles calls "fooling the left brain"—that is, bypassing the rational "common sense" part of the mind, in the process of discovering what you *really* want to do and what is God's will for you. You will notice that these exercises necessarily involve lifestyle characteristics as well as career issues. Read them over. Find a quiet place and time to do as many as you choose. And then turn to the next section of this chapter to interpret what you have written in the context of defining the ministry you are seeking.

Exercise 1: Things That Bug Me

Take a piece of paper. List all the things that bug you about your present church. These might include the people you work with, the community you live in, or the congregation's expectations of the minister. Keep writing until you run out of things that bug you.

Exercise 2: A Perfect Day

Imagine that it is five years from now. You have achieved the kind of ministry you have always dreamed of. In addition, your personal life is fulfilling, satisfying, and stimulating. You are writing to a friend in Europe, describing a typical day in your life. Describe what your office looks like, who you have lunch with, how you spend your time, what you look forward to when you get home from work, and anything else that seems important to you. Be as specific as possible.

Exercise 3: When I Am Retired . . .

This is a variation on the exercise above. Imagine that you are now retired from the active ministry. You have moved to the type of community you have always wanted to live in, and you are now spending your time in activities that are pleasurable. You also are involved part-time in the church, performing those aspects of ministry you really enjoy and that might have tended to be crowded out during your busy days of active ministry. Describe a typical day in your retirement, noting your activities both in the church and in the community.

Exercise 4: My Greatest Achievements

Look back to what you consider your three most significant achievements, in or out of the church. These are achievements in which you took a sense of personal pride and for which others have given you recognition as well. Write a short paragraph about each. Tell what you did, and note the particular abilities or strengths of personality that contributed to the achievement. A hint to get started: Divide your life into five-year segments and describe one significant achievement from each; when you are done, select the three most significant of these.

Exercise 5: Mentors and Role Models

Reflect on the individuals who exerted a formative influence upon your decision to enter the ministry or the style of ministry that you adopted. These people may have been either within or outside the institutional church. Write a short descriptive paragraph about each, noting especially what you admire about them and which of their qualities or lifestyle characteristics you have tried to emulate.

IDENTIFYING PATTERNS

Now that you have completed one or more of the exercises above, your next step is to discern the common threads or patterns that run through what you have written and, consequently, that run through your ministry as a whole. The following questions are designed to help you do that.

Exercise 1: Things That Bug Me

Read over your list. Ask yourself one basic question: These frustrations you mention—are they *situational*, or are they inherent in the nature of the work itself? By situational, I mean, are they the result of circumstances peculiar to your current position, or are they characteristic of the profession as a whole? A low salary, relative to other clergy salaries is, for example, a *situational* problem. Leave the situation (i.e., your current position) for a higher paying position, and you have solved the problem.

Problems inherent in the nature of the work itself, however, are a different matter. If you list, for example, "dealing with difficult people" as a characteristic of your present ministry, it is important to realize that you will always have to deal with difficult people in ministry (or in any employment that engages people).

Read over your entire list, therefore, and ask yourself whether the nature of the problems you list suggest leaving your present *situation* as the best solution, or whether they suggest changing the focus of your entire profession, and perhaps considering nonparish, or even secular employment.

Now take this exercise one step further. Draw a second column on your sheet. In this column, list the opposite of the negative quality you listed in column one. For example, if you listed in column one the following as a frustration of your present position: "Lack of openness in the congregation to considering new forms of liturgy." Then you might list as an opposite in column two: "Openness to new forms of

33

liturgical expression and willingness to change established forms of worship."

When you have finished, take a pair of scissors and cut each item in column two into its own separate sheet. (Though the physical act of cutting is cathartic, you can do the same thing with columns in your word processor.) Now rearrange them in their order of importance to you. When you are finished, carefully read over the first five to seven positive qualities. You are now looking at a job description for your next ministry!

Exercise 2: A Perfect Day

Read over the description of your "perfect day." Ask yourself, What kind of activities in or out of the church seem to draw forth your most enthusiastic involvement? Related to this, What is the nature of the activity in which you are personally involved when you most enjoy spending time with parishioners? Are you teaching them? Counseling with them? Visiting them?

Second, in what environment does this "perfect day" take place? What type of community are you living in? What part of the country? Finally, how many of your activities on the "perfect day" take place outside the church? Depending upon the answer to this last question, do you need to consider bivocational ministry, or even secular employment during the next stage of your professional life?

Exercise 3: When I Am Retired . . .

A variation on the exercise above, "When I Am Retired," focuses on what you *like* to do in the church, as opposed to what you *have* to do to "pay the rent"!

Look at the types of church activities in which you see yourself enjoyably involved during your retirement. These provide an important clue to discern the type and style of ministry you desire. Look also at larger lifestyle issues. What will be your hobbies and leisure time activities in retirement? Could these be more fully integrated into your leisure or professional life right now? Finally, look at the nature of the community in which you see yourself living. Is this perhaps the type of community you could target for your next church?

Exercise 4: My Greatest Achievements

A sense of achievement is highly motivating. Whatever you were doing to experience a sense of achievement in the past, you probably are motivated to perform similar achievements in the future.

To identify your achievement pattern, ask yourself some common-sense questions. In what *area of activity* were you involved when you experienced a significant sense of achievement? Was it teaching and learning? Personal involvement with one other individual? Drama or liturgies? Public speaking? Second, what was your *personal role* in this achievement? Was it as a teacher? An organizer? A counselor? Finally, what was the *result* of this achievement? Why was this achievement important in your own eyes, and why would you, therefore, be highly motivated to repeat it again in the future?

Exercise 5: Mentors and Role Models

Read over your descriptions of people who have exerted a formative influence upon you in shaping the style of your ministry or of your life as a whole. Ask yourself what major characteristics all these people have in common. Is it the *setting* in which they lived or worked—perhaps as pastors of thriving big-city churches, for example? Was it a *subject area* in which all were involved, such as music or liturgy or pastoral counseling? Or was it some element of personal style they all had in common with which you strongly identified? Whatever characteristics your mentors and role models had in common, it is likely that these qualities will continue to be an important part of your desired future ministry.

If the exercises above have worked for you, you should be starting to become aware of some strong patterns operating in your ministry, patterns that suggest the nature of your "call within the call," as well as the type of ministry you are seeking in the future. We turn now to the second subject of this chapter—identifying the *environment* best suited to express your sense of call.

YOUR BEST ENVIRONMENT

Where could your call be best expressed? For clergy currently serving in the active ministry or about to graduate from seminary, options include:

■ senior pastor
■ staff or associate pastor
■ chaplaincy or other specialized ministry
■ bivocational ministry
■ secular employment

We will now look at the requirements and characteristics of each. As we do so, consider the nature of your particular call, as it was revealed in the exercises in the first part of this chapter.

Senior Pastor

Within this category exist a variety of ministry styles. The style is determined by the pastor's own interests and abilities, the history and expectations of the congregation, the size of the church, and the socioeconomic characteristics of its members and the community in which it is located. Let us look first at size as a determinant of pastoral leadership style.

Church Size

It is likely that most ministers harbor the desire to serve a bigger church at some point in their career. However, it is important to realize that different sizes of churches call for different leadership styles. A big church is not simply a small church writ large! Different church sizes, the pastoral leadership style they require, and the approximate number of churches represented by each, were described a decade ago by church consultant Lyle Schaller as follows, below.[3] Since Schaller wrote, the trend toward increasing numbers of Americans worshiping in large or very large churches, with 500 to 1,000 or more in attendance every Sunday, has increased.

Small Church

Less than 100 in attendance. Approximately two thirds of all North American churches. The pastor is a "people person," a "shepherd" rather than a "rancher."[4] The pastoral leadership style is relationship-oriented, rather than program-oriented.

Middle-sized Church

Between 100 and 500 at worship. Approximately one quarter of all churches. The pastor functions as facilitator and enabler, with an emphasis on developing, maintaining, and nurturing lay leadership.

Large Church

Five hundred or more in worship. Less than 10 percent of all churches, but represents more than 25 percent of total church membership. The pastor functions as a "rancher," rather than a "shepherd," acting as "chief of staff," with "command" responsibilities for a large and complex organization.

Growing Church/Mission Developer

Membership size variable but growing. Requires an enterprising individual with an entrepreneurial streak, independent and self-sufficient. The pastor is an optimistic problem-solver and a self-starter, with a strong desire to succeed; a "transformational" leader.

The majority of clergy are temperamentally suited to express one or two of these styles of ministry effectively throughout their career. Competence in the leadership style required for one church size does not necessarily transfer into competence for another. The "shepherd" and "people person" of the small church is a very different role from the CEO and chief of staff of the large church. Some clergy would feel uncomfortable and constrained *until* they "move up." Other clergy would feel uncomfortable and "out of their league" *when* they move up. Ultimately, *you* must be the judge of which pastoral style is most consistent with your sense of call, based upon your own temperamental needs, and not overlooking your preferred theology of Christian community.

Read over the exercises you wrote in connection with the last part of the chapter. Ask yourself, What seems to be the nature of my preferred pastoral leadership style and, on the basis of this, what size would seem to be indicated for my next church? If you do perceive the call to move, what changes would you need to make in your existing leadership style, in order to serve a significantly larger congregation? Finally, consider your stage in ministry. Some clergy prefer to move to a church of the same size (a "lateral move"), or even smaller, during their last few years before retirement.

Socioeconomic Environment

The socioeconomic characteristic of church members, and also of the community in which the church is located, is another important factor to be considered in identifying the best setting in which to express your sense of call. Ministry to a blue-collar congregation requires a different style and rhetoric, for example, from ministry to managerial and professional people.[5] It is probably fair to say that a majority of clergy prefer to serve people whose background and interests are similar to their own.

Again, read over your exercises and ask yourself, on the basis of your interests, abilities, and preferred leadership style, what would seem to be the socioeconomic background of the congregation best suited to your sense of call?

Staff Position

A position as staff member or pastoral associate at a large church is worth considering for clergy right out of seminary who are still "learning the ropes," and also for more experienced clergy who want to express a more specialized ministry. If your exercises reflect a strong interest in one or two specialized areas of ministry, along with a relative disinterest in *administering* a church, then serving as a pastoral associate may be the role for you.

Specialized Ministry

Some clergy feel a strong call to express particular *aspects* of ministry (counseling, for example) or to work with particular *populations groups* (young people, or prisoners, hospital patients, or older people in an institutional setting, for example). Options for specialized ministry, besides serving as a staff member or pastoral associate at a large church, or as chaplain to an institution, include serving in a staff position on the denominational level, in a religious publishing house, and even in self-employment. Self-employment beyond the local church is especially well-suited to those who feel a call to serve as pastoral counselors.

Some clergy have even succeeded in "inventing" their own ministry. One pastor of my acquaintance has created a ministry by educating church members about the third world. Another travels around the country, presenting programs on liturgy and drama. Others, who formerly might have opened a religious bookshop, are entering the world of telecommunications, publishing, and interactive media, as the technology explodes all around us. If the idea of inventing your own ministry appeals to you, you need to possess well-developed business and organizational skills, along with a strong interest in one or two specialized areas of ministry.

Bivocational Ministry

Another way to express your call is to work part-time in the church and part-time in some area outside the church. A typical example might be the minister of a small church who works part-time as associate in a pastoral-counseling agency or teaches in the local school. This style of ministry is inevitable and will become increasingly common in the future, as clergy struggle with the tension of being overeducated and underemployed, in small and financially marginal churches.

Secular Employment

Secular employment may be a real option for clergy who desire a radical change from parish ministry, who need more income than the church can provide, or who believe that their own particular gifts, abilities, and interests can be best expressed *outside* the church and its publics. We will look at the challenges that face clergy contemplating secular employment, as well as its potential advantages, in chapter 11.

YOUR "MARKETABILITY"

In this chapter, we have been defining your sense of call as it relates to the nature of the ministry you hope to obtain. The next step is to identify the type of position you can reasonably expect to be offered, on the basis of your previous "track record" and other factors. On the one hand, you want to guard against unrealistic expectations. On the other hand, you do not want to devalue yourself and avoid pursuing positions for which, in reality, you are well qualified. In seeking a new call, how can you realistically assess your own "marketability"?

Your marketability depends upon several factors. Among the most important are the following:

- Your current level of responsibility—the size of the church you presently serve and your position in it, whether as senior pastor or staff associate.
- Your previous "track record"—what you have accomplished in your present and immediate past ministries, as measured primarily in quantitative terms: new membership, budget increases, and so on.
- How effectively you present yourself in an interview.
- Personal factors—these include age, gender, and marital status.
- Absence of negative factors—these might include a recent divorce, a history of job instability, having recently been terminated or forced to resign under pressure from your present church, or a past history of scandal or impropriety.

In order to assess your marketability in the context of factors such as those listed above, speak to your denominational placement officer or supervisor. This person should be able to give you a realistic assessment of the size and type of church or other ministry you should be targeting.

Also, ask yourself some hard-nosed questions: What *is* your "track record" in your present position? Answer in *quantitative* terms: budget increase, membership increase, new groups started, and such. Research some actual figures, if necessary. These will be helpful to you when you get to the interview. Also, how well *do* you present yourself in an interview? *Do* you have a relative absence of negative factors in your background (i.e., a recent divorce), *or,* if you do have one or more negatives, are they offset by some strong positive factors (i.e., an unusually strong record of accomplishment in your present ministry)?

As a general rule, for clergy interested in "moving up," a reasonable goal would be to target churches with budgets 50 to 100 percent greater than that of your present church. If your present church has a budget of $100,000, for example, you will target churches in the $150,000–$200,000 range.

MINISTRY-GOAL STATEMENT

In this chapter, you have defined the nature of your call as you currently perceive it, and you have identified ministry opportunities consistent with that call. The next step is to summarize the goals for your new ministry, in the form of a ministry-goal statement. A ministry-goal statement has two purposes:

■ It will serve as a guide for you as you seek new positions.

■ It will provide the basis for the ministry statement or philosophy of ministry, on your minister's information sheet and/or résumé.

In preparing to write a ministry-goal statement:

■ Read over the exercises you have completed for this chapter.

■ Notice repeated words and phrases.

When you find that you repeatedly have said the same thing in different ways, then you are discovering some basic elements of your ministry pattern.

■ Summarize the results in a ministry-goal statement.

Your ministry-goal statement should describe: (1) the nature of the position you are seeking; (2) the gifts you would bring to it; and (3) any other ministry-related or lifestyle-related characteristics you consider important. Examples might include the following:

■ To serve as senior pastor of a medium to large church that is interested in increasing membership and enhancing stewardship.

■ To serve as part-time associate pastor, with responsibilities for Christian education and outreach, in a church located in a rural or semirural area of the northeast.

■ To serve as executive director of a church-related community-service agency, with emphasis upon staff training and development, grant writing, and new program development.

PLACEMENT MATERIALS

In this chapter, you have defined the nature of your call, identified ministry opportunities consistent with it, and written a ministry-goal statement to guide you as you move into the search process. We turn now to the next step—preparing placement materials to help you achieve the position you desire and to which God is calling you, during this next stage of your ministry.

Chapter Four

PREPARING YOUR MATERIALS

Even if I boast a little . . . our hope is that . . .
we may preach the gospel in lands beyond.

II Corinthians 10:8a, 15b, 16a (RSV)

Knowledge of what you want is the first step in the placement process. Presenting it on paper is the second step.

Your placement materials are *not* just a "work biography." They are the means by which you "sell" yourself to a prospective church, either directly or through established systems.

If you have prepared your placement materials effectively, a member of a search committee or pastor-parish committee reading them should be able to say, "If we call this individual, these are the gifts and abilities they will bring to our church." These gifts and abilities, of course, may or may not be what that particular church needs (this will be up to the search committee and others to decide), but at least the church will have an accurate sense of your gifts, based upon the materials you supply.

In this chapter, we will look at your written placement materials, including your Minister's Information Form, résumé, correspondence to and from churches or executives, and other supplementary materials. We turn first to some general guidelines.

PRESENTING YOURSELF ON PAPER

In preparing to write your materials, remind yourself of the dual purpose of these placement documents—not only (1) to get a new call, but (2) to get the *right* call. *Getting* a call has to do with presenting yourself and your ministry as effectively as possible. Getting the *right* call has to do with being *selective* in deciding which aspects of your ministry you choose to emphasize, even if the end result may narrow the range of possibilities you may encounter.

Before you begin, give yourself some time and "space," so that you can reflect quietly and prayerfully on the ministry to which you believe God is calling you. After you have completed the first draft of your

43

materials, put them aside for a few days. Then take them out again and read them with fresh eyes. Give them to a trusted colleague, or to a layperson who has recently served on a pastor-nominating committee, and ask for their reaction. When you are satisfied that your materials present a clear and accurate picture of the ministry you wish to offer a congregation, then you are ready to send them out.

THE PASTOR'S PROFILE

Called by such names as Pastor's Profile, Personal Profile, Personal Information Form, Ministerial Profile, Ministerial Record Sheet, or Relocation Assistance Form, and ranging in length from a one-page computer printout used by the Episcopal and American Baptist churches, to a five- or six-page narrative form used by some other denominations, the purpose of the Ministerial Profile is to communicate the experience, gifts, and abilities that you would bring to a new position.

The general appearance of your profile is extremely important. Make sure the information you present is neat, legible, and concise. Pay particular attention to correct spelling and punctuation. Avoid theological jargon, because the information you present will be read primarily by laypeople. Use good quality paper for supplementary sheets, and type with a new black or carbon ribbon. Use "white space" in margins, between paragraphs, and between questions. *Condense* what you are saying, rather than trying to jam too much material into a small space. Your denomination may give you the choice of printing or typing/keystroking information. It is best to use a *typewriter* or *word processor*. A hand-printed form, no matter how neat, does not convey the same professional appearance as a typed form.

Consider in detail the specific information requested on most pastor's profiles.

Basic Information

Make sure the information you supply in this section is accurate and up-to-date. It would be embarrassing to have you listed with the wrong spouse! If you have acquired additional degrees or other qualifications since your last update, make sure those are listed as well.

Education

Remember to include your continuing education, as well as completed degree programs. Under continuing education, you also can list participation in one- or two-day workshops and seminars. If a particular ministry topic was discussed as part of a clergy conference you attended, list this as well. If you have participated in little or no continuing education, include your personal reading on selected ministry topics as a "self-study."

Position Desired

Be honest in describing the nature of the position you are seeking. Don't worry about being too restrictive, in terms of your expressed desires, in the early stages of your search. If your goals are unrealistic, your denominational placement officer will undoubtedly let you know. The important thing is that this section of your profile presents a clear picture of the position you are really seeking and are prepared to accept.

Pastoral Specialties

Identify areas of ministry in which you not only excel but also enjoy. Don't list what you believe to be "hot" areas of ministry, in the expectation that this will make you more employable. Instead, communicate a sense of the ministry you enjoy, and to which you believe God is calling you.

Work Experience

List your present and immediate past positions. You usually will be asked to do this in reverse chronological order. If you are asked to indicate accomplishments, be specific. Members of a search committee will be more impressed with a statement that, under your leadership, the church increased its average weekly attendance 25 percent during the past five years, than with a vague statement that the congregation "increased its spiritual growth." (If spiritual growth is the measure, then it is better to say that xx number of people participated in discipleship programs x, y, and z.)

Make sure that the nature of the accomplishments you cite are consistent with the nature of the position you are seeking. In other words, if you are laying claim to being a pastor who gets things done the right way, you will want to cite accomplishments as measured by church growth, evangelism, and new-member incorporation.

Leadership Style

Called variously a Work Orientation Description or an Evaluation of Work Style, this is an important part of your profile. Search committees often use this section as a guide for interviewing. In general, avoid extremes of response. If you are conservative theologically, and do want to communicate this, but in a nonthreatening manner, choose the second-highest response on the grid. That way, you will indicate your general theological orientation without the danger of presenting yourself as an extremist.

Involvements Outside the Congregation

List activities in your immediate community, membership on denominational committees and commissions, and, if asked, hobbies and leisure activities. Be careful not to give the impression that you are overcommitted outside the church.

When listing denominational and other involvements, emphasize those that relate to the areas of ministry you are claiming. If you are claiming gifts in evangelism, then membership on the denominational evangelism committee will be a big plus. Avoid listing hobbies unless you are specifically asked to do so. Your particular interest may be a negative feature to a member of the search committee. Instead, emphasize ministry-related activities in the community and in the denomination.

Special Concerns

This is a catch-all category, in which you may address such issues as special health or educational concerns of family members, or circumstances of a spouse's employment that might affect your availability for a new position.

In general, avoid bringing up potential negative and/or restricting factors that might better be addressed in an interview. If a special circumstance surrounding your candidacy is that you are currently unemployed as a result of having been forced to resign from your present church, request your denomination's settlement director to write an addendum to your Ministerial Profile, stating the nature of the circumstances under which you were working, and what you were able to accomplish in the congregation in spite of the difficulties you encountered.

Ministry Statement

This is the most important part of your profile. Called variously Statement on the Church and Ministry, Introductory Statement, or Personal Narrative, this statement is the most effective way for you to communicate the essence of the ministry you offer. The contents should function as a summary of the pastoral specialties you claim, and should be consistent with the ministry-goal statement you wrote when you read the previous chapter of this book. After reading your "statement," a search committee should have a clear picture of who you are, both as a person and as a pastor.

In composing your statement, the rules of fine writing apply. Don't be long-winded. Don't be boring. Avoid theological jargon. Begin paragraphs with a topic sentence. Use "action verbs." Begin sentences with such phrases as "I am . . . I do . . . ." Focus on specific accomplishments, supported by statistics wherever possible. Use brief vignettes to illustrate major accomplishments. In drafting your final copy, make sure that spelling, punctuation, and grammar are correct.

References

Be sure to include the names of one or two key laypeople. It is your lay references that will tend to carry the most weight. If your search is confidential, indicate on your form that your lay references are to be contacted only if a church is seriously considering your candidacy. If you are hoping to relocate to another section of the country, seek out references in that area, if possible.

In selecting references, choose people who have known you and worked with you for the past few years, rather than people who have known you since the earliest days of your ministry. People who have known you for a long time will tend to say that they have seen you "grow" in ministry. This may make you sound immature to prospective search committee members. Instead, choose individuals who currently work with you and can speak of your current abilities.

Before listing an individual, be sure to ask if they are willing to serve as a reference, and also supply them with adequate information about the requirements of the position you are seeking, as well as about your gifts and abilities for ministry as you perceive them. Be sure to communicate a sense of this also to your denominational placement officer. Do not assume that people know enough about you and your ministry to serve as effective references without some tactful "coaching" on your part.

In general, the more informed your references are about the nature of the positions you are seeking, as well as about the gifts and abilities you claim, the more effective they will be in presenting you as the right candidate for positions in which you are interested.

THE RÉSUMÉ

In most denominations, the Clergy Profile functions as a résumé. For some denominations, however, and for some individual churches, you may be requested to send a résumé along with your Profile and other placement materials.

When preparing an effective résumé, you should be clear about its purpose. A résumé is not simply a "work history" (sometimes called a vitae). A résumé is better understood as a marketing tool, designed to present your skills and previous experience in such a manner that you may be considered for particular opportunities in the future. In other words, a résumé is a *selective distillation* of pastoral gifts and previous professional experience.

Chronological Résumé

The two basic types of résumés have both strengths and weaknesses. More common is the *chronological résumé*, which lists, in reverse chronological order, the positions you have held, along with your responsibilities for each position, in a manner similar to this:

1988 to Present	*St. Andrew's Church,* Oak Grove, Minn., senior pastor, in charge of a church of 350 members, with three paid staff.
1984 to 1987	*St. Luke's Church,* New Bedford, Conn., associate pastor, director of the Christian education program.
1982 to 1984	*Grace Church,* Maple Bluffs, N.J., assistant pastor, leader of youth outreach.

The problem with a chronological résumé, however, is that while it effectively presents a clear picture of your employment history, it often does not communicate a clear sense of your particular gifts and abilities.

Functional Résumé

In order to address the problem of the chronological résumé, some people recommend the use of a *functional résumé,* which lists skill areas demonstrated by prior employment, like this:

Preaching
- Taught homiletics in district-sponsored lay school of theology
- Wrote an article, "Principles of Dynamic Preaching," for national denominational publication.
- Increased church attendance 50 percent through effective preaching while senior pastor of St. Andrew's, Oak Grove.

A functional résumé would then go on to list two or three additional pastoral specialties, such as stewardship, Christian education, program development, or counseling, along with particular accomplishments under each.

The problem with a functional résumé, however, is that while it presents a clear picture of your gifts and abilities, it is less effective in communicating an accurate sense of the chronology of your employment history.

Combination Chronological and Functional Résumé

To combine the best qualities of both the chronological and the functional résumé, some clergy placement professionals suggest that pastors write a chronological résumé, with pastoral specialties indicated by means of specific accomplishments listed under each position, such as the following:

1987 to Present	St. Andrew's Church, Oak Grove, Minn., senior pastor. Active *preaching ministry,* including increasing church attendance by means of effective sermons.
1984 to 1987	St. Luke's Church, New Bedford, Conn., associate pastor. Development of the church's *educational ministry* by designing new-member courses, teaching adult Bible, and conducting educational outreach in the community.
1982 to 1984	Grace Church, Maple Bluffs, N.J., assistant pastor. Leadership in *youth ministry,* as developer and facilitator of programs for junior and senior high.

Probably a still better way to combine the best qualities of the functional and chronological résumé has been suggested by author Yana Parker in her excellent book, *The Damn Good Résumé Guide.*[1] On the next two pages is an example of the model Parker suggests, as it might be written by a pastor seeking a new position. Read it over carefully. Note the comments in the various section on the first page. Then use it as a model to write your own résumé.

Keep personal information simple;
for confidentiality, you may want to
use your home address and phone as
the contact.

Summarize your sense of call. Be specific. Describe the nature of the position you are looking for, as expressed in terms of the needs of the church or other employing organization, rather than your own personal needs.

List 3 to 5 items which summarize the
essence of the ministry you would
bring to a new call. Make sure the
items you list are consistent with your
Ministry Objective and your Pastoral
Specialties.

Use action verbs to describe your most significant accomplishments under each of 3 or 4 pastoral specialties. Cite specific facts and figures whenever possible. Include also significant accomplishments outside the church.

List work experience in reverse
chronological order, starting with
the present. Note church size
and/or particular areas of responsibility, if important.

You can also list workshops, seminars, and other non-degree programs, especially as they relate to the Pastoral Specialities you claim.

DONALD J. PASTOR
29 Glen View Drive
Providence RI 02903
(401) 995-1884

MINISTRY OBJECTIVE

Senior Pastor of a program-size congregation with a need for enhanced stewardship, program development, and new member incorporation.

SUMMARY OF QUALIFICATIONS

- 1 years experience in congregational ministry
- Increased stewardship in present church 50% in 5 years
- Led congregation in a major programmatic expansion
- D.Min. in evangelism and new-member incorporation

PASTORAL SPECIALTIES

Stewardship
- Increased giving in present church 10% a year for each of the last 5 years
- Designed a stewardship education program now used in 6 area churches
- Chaired denominational stewardship committee for last 3 years

Program Development
- Added a senior high group to the youth program
- Started the first men's group in the church
- Expanded the church's outreach program

New-Member Incorporation
- Initiated a newcomer lay visitation program
- Increased attendance 25% over the past 5 years by improving incorporation procedures
- Wrote an article, "The User Friendly Church," for the July/August 1993 issue of *Your Church*

EMPLOYMENT HISTORY

1987—Present   SENIOR PASTOR—St. Andrew's, Providence, R.I.
- 300 members, 3 paid staff, $118,000 budget

1984–87   ASSOCIATE PASTOR—St. Luke's, Barrington, R.I.
- Shared responsibility for general congregational ministry

1981–84   ASSISTANT—Grace, Maple Bluffs, N.J.
- Responsible for Christian education and youth ministry

EDUCATION

D.MIN., Andover Newton Theological School, Newton Centre, Mass., 1988 (Area of special focus: New-member incorporation)

M.DIV., General Theological Seminary, New York, N.Y., 1981

B.A., Muhlenberg College, Allentown, Penna., 1972

When composing your résumé, remember to keep it tight and focused. The average person spends 30 to 60 seconds reading a résumé, so your résumé needs to make a strong initial impression. In length, one page is recommended, but two is allowable. Obviously, a pastor with twenty years experience in ministry has more to list than someone just out of seminary.

When you are finished, ask a knowledgeable person to critique it. Someone who has recently served on a pastoral search committee would be especially insightful.

When you are satisfied that your résumé presents a clear picture of your ministry, type it with a clean ribbon, or use a word processor, and have it reproduced on white or cream-colored matte (not shiny) paper. The original copy can be typed on an IBM Selectric (the "Letter Gothic" type style is both readable and compact) or on an Apple Macintosh computer (MacWrite software) in Geneva font, or the DOS equivalent. Professional typesetting is usually not necessary for a résumé for church positions, and might even make you come across as "too slick." For reproduction, the Kodak and Xerox 9500 reproduce on paper with a matte (not shiny) finish. Reproduce a two-page résumé front and back on the same sheet.

The Résumé and Special Circumstances

You may have special circumstances surrounding your candidacy which would affect the preparation of your résumé. You may be pursuing two or more different *kinds* of ministry objectives simultaneously, or, if you are a late vocation, preparing to enter the ministry for the first time.

If you are pursuing two or more ministry objectives—pastor of a local church *or* denominational staff position, for example—it is best to prepare two or more *different* résumés. As time consuming as it may be, preparing multiple résumés is the only way to emphasize the gifts, abilities, and experience appropriate for each position.

If you are a late vocation, preparing to enter the active ministry for the first time, emphasize whatever church-related experience you have (seminary fieldwork, for example), and, when listing secular work, emphasize those aspects of your previous employment that have relevance to church ministry. If you were once named your company's Sales Representative of the Year, for example, this has obvious relevance to your ability to relate to people, and also offers evidence of communication skills that might be employed in evangelism, which will be noted by the members of a search committee!

Supplementary Materials

Your ministerial packet and/or résumé are your basic placement documents. However, supplementary materials from clergy may be requested, or clergy may choose to submit such documents to augment their candidacy. In general, unless these materials are of unusually high quality, or unless they are specifically requested, it is wise to rely on your official placement documents to convey a strong initial impression of your ministry. Supplementary materials, however, may include the following:

Sermons. If sending sermons, keep in mind that there is no substitute for hearing you preach in person. If, however, you do send sermons, you must decide whether to send them in written form (no more than three in number) or as audiotapes or videotapes (one would be sufficient). What you send should be characteristic of your preaching style, as well as sermon content. An audiotape recorded from the congregation, rather than from the pulpit, will give a better sense of congregational reaction to what you are saying. The best form for communicating a sense of your preaching style, as well as congregational reaction to it, would be a videotape in which the camera operator pans around the congregation from time to time.

Church Newsletters. Include these only if they are of unusually high quality (few are; desktop publishing programs are allowing for improvement), or if they point to some innovative and/or highly successful church program.

Autobiography. You may already have written an autobiography, or "spiritual journey," in the Statement on Ministry section of your ministerial packet. An autobiography or spiritual journey may serve to "humanize" you in the eyes of some prospective search committee members. However, it may also unintentionally contain elements that turn off one or more of its members, and therefore eliminate you from consideration in an early stage of a search. Use spiritual autobiographies with extreme caution, if at all.

Testimonials or Letters of Reference. Do not include these in your basic packet unless there is some particular reason for doing so. Let the search committee do its own reference checking.

Photographs. Usually, it is not advisable or necessary to include photographs of yourself or your family. Do so only if you present an attractive appearance, and submit only professional quality studio photographs—no backyard specials.

Finding the Vacancies: Filling the Need

You are now ready to begin the active phase of your search. Your paperwork is complete. You have clearly defined the nature of the position you want—the type of ministry to which you believe God is calling you.

You are now ready to begin the next step in the process, working within the procedures of your denomination to identify potential churches and to have your materials placed before them.

THE SEARCH BEGINS . . .

You have now completed your basic placement documents and are prepared to move into the active phase of your search. The first step is to contact churches.

Corresponding with Churches

Depending upon your denomination's polity regarding whether pastors are allowed to initiate contact with prospective churches, you may be sending letters to open congregations, expressing an interest in being considered as a candidate. In denominations where such conduct is not encouraged, the correspondence would be channeled through a gatekeeper. The purpose of your letter of inquiry, or "cover letter," is threefold:

■ To express interest in the position;

■ To spark *their* interest in you as a candidate;

■ To invite them to take the next step—usually, invite you for an interview.

On the next two pages is a sample cover letter. Read it over, as you did the sample résumé, and note the comments. Then use it as a model for writing your own letter to prospective churches or placement executives.

Questionnaires

Once you have expressed an interest in candidating for a church, you may be asked to respond in writing to a questionnaire drafted by the church. Most of the questions you will encounter in the typical church questionnaire will be of a general nature, such as:

• What is your philosophy of ministry?

What to include on your . . .

Address it to a specific person, not just "Chair of the Search Committee."

Convey excitement and enthusiasm about the position by pointing to something specific that they obviously feel good about.

Point to an area of personal strength that relates to an expressed congregational goal on their profile. Use the cover letter to supplement the contents of your official deployment documents.

Use the cover letter to explain any special circumstances in your present ministry that impacts on your record of achievement. The message here is, "I succeeded in expanding the ministry of this church in spite of the impediments."

Include a personal touch, if appropriate and relevant. This says, "I know your area. I won't lose time adjusting to living in a new area if I am called."

Gently urge them to take the next step in the deployment process regarding your candidacy.

Note enclosures on your letter. This reminds you of what materials you have sent to the church.

... Cover Letter

October 1, 1993

Mr. John Jones, Chairman
Search Committee
Newington Community Church
151 Maple Avenue
Newington, Connecticut 02791

Dear Mr. Jones:

I would like to express an interest in being considered for the position of senior pastor at Newington Community Church.

In reading your profile, I was impressed by your church's commitment to stewardship and by your expressed desire to make further progress in this area. I believe that I possess gifts and experience you may want to consider. As senior pastor of Westerly Road Community Church, a growing congregation in Providence, Rhode Island, I have led the congregation in an intensive program of stewardship education. The result has been an increase in giving, an average of 10 percent a year for each of the past five years.

In addition to stewardship, my ministry also stresses program development and new-member incorporation, which you indicated on your profile to be of prime importance for your church. My present church has increased service attendance significantly during the past five years, in spite of the fact that the community in which we are located is of stable population, and primarily Roman Catholic.

Although I have served churches in Rhode Island and in New Jersey since my ordination eleven years ago, I am familiar with the Newington area, having taught in your region prior to entering seminary. My wife's family is also native to Rhode Island.

I look forward to hearing from you.

In Faith,

(The Rev.) Donald J. Pastor

Enclosures: Pastor's Profile, résumé, sermon tape

- What are your leadership strengths and weaknesses as you perceive them?
- What is your attitude toward lay ministry? How have you supported it in the past?

In addition to these general questions, one or two very specific questions may be directed to you, clearly pointing to areas of concern in the life of the congregation. Before responding to a church questionnaire, ask yourself why these particular questions are being asked. Then respond with a high degree of sensitivity, but also with candor. If, as a result of your honest answers to a questionnaire, you are eliminated from consideration, you probably were not meant to go to that particular church in the first place.

Responding to the questionnaires of several different churches over a period of weeks or months can be extremely time consuming. However, possibly half the questions you are asked will appear in a slightly different form on another church questionnaire. Therefore, save copies of your responses, and alter and adapt your responses when corresponding with subsequent churches. If you have a computer, you can store your responses on disk for future use.

The Contributions Document

A Contributions Document, in which you summarize what you see as your major achievements in the congregation, can be excellent preparation for an interview, as well as for preparing your basic placement materials. In order to prepare a Contributions Document, simply divide a piece of paper into three columns as shown below:

Contributions	Examples of Skills	Qualifications

Under "Contributions," write some five-to-ten-word summaries of your most significant achievements in the church. Under "Skills," note personal qualities or skill areas which contributed to each achievement, such as perseverance, creativity, goal-setting, or strategic planning. Under "Qualifications," list any particular expertise you possess which contributed to your significant achievement, such as the completion of a degree program or of a seminar or workshop in a selected topic area.

Many clergy have found filling out a Contributions Document an invaluable preparation for an interview.

Record Keeping

As your search enters its active phase, and depending upon your denomination's polity regarding how aggressively you are able to initiate contact with potential churches, you may find yourself actively involved with half a dozen to a dozen churches in various stages of the search process. You should keep track of where you are with each one, and also of any important deadlines coming up.

Maintain a file folder for each church, containing copies of correspondence sent and received, as well as notes of telephone conversations. In addition, record reminders on your calendar of tasks to be performed, such as:

> October 14: Contact search committee at St. Mark's.
> (It is now a month since I last heard.)

Finally, maintain professional standards throughout the search and respond promptly to all correspondence. Consider sending requested materials by FAX or overnight mail. This will demonstrate an interest in the position and help to get you noticed among several competing candidates.

If You Don't Hear

If you have sent out your placement materials and nothing seems to be happening, remember that the search process does take a long time. If, however, you feel that the process is taking longer than normal, or if you seem to be receiving an unusual number of rejections early on in the process, look again at your placement materials and at the references you have chosen. Ask yourself some basic questions:

- Is my profile as a whole effectively presenting me as a candidate?
- Are *parts* of the profile overly restrictive? (Look especially at your minimum salary requirements and geographic preference.)
- Are my references carefully selected, and are they sharing supportive information about me? (If necessary, phone one or two of your references and try to get a sense of the information they are sharing about you.)

Make changes on your profile or in your reference list, as needed, and then continue your search.

We turn now to the topic of identifying potential opportunities for ministry.

Chapter Five

IDENTIFYING VACANCIES

I said, "Here am I; send me!"

Isaiah 6:8*b*

Once you have defined the nature of the call you are seeking and have prepared your placement materials, you are ready to choose whom you will serve, by working within the placement procedures of your denomination.

Placement Methods

Three basic placement methods are used in the church.[1] Which of the three is used by a particular denomination is determined by its polity, based on its historic understanding of the nature of ministry, and of the role of authority in the church. The three placement methods are:

Open Method

Found in the Baptist bodies, the Church of God, Christian Church (Disciples of Christ), and United Church of Christ. Ministers take the initiative in using available denominational resources and are free to negotiate terms with the congregation.

Restricted Open Method

Found in the Presbyterian bodies, The Episcopal Church, Lutheran groups, the Reformed Church in America, and the Church of the Nazarene. Ministers are provided with a greater degree of assistance on the judicatory level. Denominational officials play a significant advisory role in the placement process, for both the pastor and the local church. The congregation chooses its pastor in accordance with eligibility guidelines determined by the judicatory.

Closed Method

Found in The United Methodist Church and in several other denominations with roots in Methodist or holiness traditions (such as the Church of God in Cleveland, Tenn.). Ministers are appointed to churches by the bishop; district superintendents play an advisory role. Ministers make their preferences known, as do congregations, but the final power of appointment belongs to the bishop.

When seeking a new position, first familiarize yourself with the placement procedure used in your denomination. (Placement procedures used in 19 of the major denominations are described in appendix A.) Knowledge of your denomination's placement procedures will tell you how much assistance you can expect to receive, and how much personal initiative you may exercise during your search.

FORMAL AND INFORMAL CHANNELS: Thirteen Ways to Find and Be Found

In every denomination, formal as well as informal channels exist for identifying available positions and for having your name presented to potential congregations. Formal channels include working with your denomination's placement officer, as well as referring to the Positions Open Bulletin, if such a publication exists in your denomination. Informal channels include a personal network of contacts to gather information about available positions.

In seeking a new position, you must decide, in advance, the degree to which it is appropriate for you to use formal or informal channels in conducting your search. As a general rule, and depending upon placement procedures used in your denomination, the following principles apply:

• For "mainstream" candidates (i.e., white males in the prime job-candidating years of the 30s and 40s), both formal and informal channels should be used.

• For women and minority candidates, who often are excluded from the informal channels, maximum use should be made of formal channels.

• For candidates who are part of emerging denominational movements or independent congregational associations, only informal channels will be available, though many of these types of pastors move in and out of denominations as they pursue their call.

Basically, there are at least thirteen channels for identifying available positions and for getting your name before a church. Not all of these will apply to your *denomination*. Not all will apply to your *situation*. As we discuss these channels, keep in mind—

> *The greater the number of channels you use,*
> *the more successful you are likely to be.*

Surveys have shown that the average job hunter uses fewer than two of the many possible methods of identifying vacant positions in the secular marketplace.[2] In a similar fashion, clergy typically rely on only two or three tried and true methods. Clergy seeking a new call need to make use of as many available channels as apply to their situation, both to increase their possibilities and to spread their search.

The thirteen ways of identifying available positions in the church include the following:

■ denominational officials and staff
■ Positions Open Bulletin
■ personal network
■ computer matching
■ vacancy-sharing consultations
■ local and regional listings
■ seminary placement listings
■ classified ads
■ clergy/church "job fairs"
■ female and minority networks and preference listings
■ special theological emphasis networks
■ opportunities in missions and aided congregations
■ ministries out of the country

Let's consider these thirteen channels in greater detail.

No. 1—Denominational Officials and Staff

Making an appointment with the appropriate denominational staff person should be your first step when seeking a new position.

Two key people must be approached on the denominational level. The first is the head of your judicatory (or the head of the judicatory in which you hope to relocate). Called variously the bishop, the district executive, the regional or area minister, or the regional executive, this person will ordinarily consult with you at the beginning of your search.

The individual you will actually work with is usually a second person on the judicatory level. Called variously the settlement director, deployment officer, consultant for ministry, or district superintendent, this person will assist in your search and act as liaison between you, the judicatory head, and the search committees of prospective churches.

When contacting denominational personnel at the beginning of your search, be clear about the nature of the position you are seeking and communicate a sense of this to the person(s) with whom you will be working.

No. 2— Positions Open Bulletin

Called, in various denominations, the Positions Open Bulletin, Church Employment Opportunities, or Pulpit Vacancies, these are monthly listings of available churches and church positions, published by several of the larger denominations. The Positions Open Bulletin is usually available by subscription, or in some cases as a free service, from a national church office. Similar "openings" bulletins are available from various academic societies for the study of religion, Scripture, preaching, liturgy, or pastoral counseling.

No. 3—Personal Network

Previously called the Old Boy Network or Good ol' Boy System, personal networks in the church are informal, word-of-mouth contacts from one pastor to another about available positions. This type of network persists in open systems, but may be even more powerful in closed systems. In addition to networking among colleagues, every pastor needs to take advantage of that wider network of family, friends, and acquaintances, lay and ordained, who can help serve as your eyes and ears during the search process. Let as wide a circle of people as possible know that you are looking, and what you are looking for.

No. 4—Computer Matching

The Episcopal Church and the American Baptist Church are two denominations which use a system of computer matching of clergy and congregations. Clergy and congregations fill out search forms, which are then matched on the basis of similar ministry goals. Congregations are mailed the profiles of clergy whose ministry goals appear to match the needs of the church.

No. 5—Vacancy-Sharing Consultations

Many denominations hold periodic regional meetings of judicatory heads and/or placement officers, in which the names of clergy seeking new positions and churches seeking new pastors are shared. If such a procedure is followed in your denomination, ask your placement officer to share your name and qualifications.

No. 6—Local and Regional Listings

In addition to national Positions Open Listings, regional listings are available as well, containing some positions which have not been listed nationally. If you have targeted your search to a particular geographic area, find out whether there is a separate Positions Open Listing for this region, and whether it could be made available to you.

No. 7—Seminary Placement Listings

Helpful primarily in assisting recent graduates to obtain their first position in the church, your seminary placement office also may carry listings of positions of interest to alumni. Contact your seminary to see if it does maintain such a list. Some alumni offices mail such notices as a service that might lead to contributions from grateful alumni who have been placed.

No. 8—Classified Ads

Some denominational publications carry notices of churches that are looking for a new minister, and ministers seeking a new call sometimes place ads in denominational magazines. If you are considering placing or responding to such ads, it is well to keep in mind a fact that career expert Richard Bolles points out—that classified ads are one of the least effective methods of bringing job seekers and employers together.[3] Churches may look askance at pastors who advertise their availability, and churches that advertise for clergy may be attempting to bypass normal denominational placement procedures. Ads are still another possible way through which clergy and churches are sometimes brought together. Independent or nondenominational churches are much more likely to use such ads for establishing the field of candidates.

No. 9—Clergy/Church "Job Fairs"

An innovative approach recently adopted by the Presbyterian Church U.S.A. is "Face to Face," one-day events in which clergy seeking a new call are brought together with representatives of churches looking for a new minister. Other denominations have not yet adopted what appears to be a very sensible idea, although the Unitarian Universalists are typical of many denominations, in that clergy and members of churches seeking a new minister meet and talk informally during the church's annual General Assembly. Clergy with doctorates who wish to receive a call or appointment to an academic position in a seminary or college often attend similar fairs at various academic societies, such as the Society of Biblical Literature or American Academy of Religion. Such positions often have more than 150 applicants competing for each opening, which means that a costly trip to such a job fair is likely to lead to poor results. Informal channels and inquiries by mentors should be tested first.

No. 10—Female and Minority Networks and Preference Listings

When responding to the difficulties that ordained women and members of minority groups experience in obtaining employment in the church, women and minorities in several denominations have formed informal, ad hoc networking groups to address issues of placement. In addition, some denominational Positions Open Bulletins note positions when applications from women and minorities are especially encouraged. Finally, some denominations have appointed staff persons on the national level to assist women and/or minorities in making the system work for them.

If you are an ordained woman and/or a member of a minority group, find out what kind of assistance—either informal or formal—is available to help you in your search.

No. 11—Special Theological Emphasis Networks

If you consider yourself "renewal-oriented," "charismatic," "liberationist," or espouse a particular theological emphasis within your denomination, you may discover that there is a network of like-minded individuals knowledgeable about vacant churches that are seeking clergy with your convictions. Speak to other like-minded people and find out whether any such network, either formal or informal, does exist in your denomination.

No. 12—Missions and Aided Congregations

Missions and "subsidized" congregations often follow quite different procedures in selecting a minister than do financially self-supporting congregations. In open or closed systems, ministers often are simply assigned to locations on the judicatory level. If your calling and defined ministry goals are oriented to church planting, or to moving a church off the plateau, or if ministry in a smaller congregation interests you, inquire from your placement officer whether any such positions are available and the procedure for being considered.

In the case of planting new churches, or if you sense a leading to revitalize a particular congregation, many judicatory decision makers are increasingly open to receiving specific proposals that are workable, knowledgeable about the community, and cost-effective. Within emerging social networks, as mainstream denominations decline in influence or ability to innovate, some larger churches of one denomination are helping to start new churches of another denomination.

The arrangements vary, from placing the start-up pastor on staff for a year, to supplying facilities and subsidizing the start-up costs. This new kind of congregational ecumenism has occurred at Wooddale Church in Minnesota and also at Chapel Hill Bible Church in North Carolina, for example.

No. 13—Ministry Out of the Country

Difficulty in obtaining employment in the U.S. is not, in itself, a sufficient reason for considering a ministry out of the country. However, if ministry out of the country does appeal to you, speak to your placement officer about how to pursue this possibility in your denomination. American clergy serving in Canada, for example, encounter a country much like ours, but with safe and livable urban centers and other attractive advantages.

As stated previously, not all thirteen ways will apply to your denomination. And not all will apply to your particular situation. But the more channels you pursue for finding out about available positions and having your name presented for consideration, the greater your chances of speeding your search and achieving your goals for this next stage of your ministry.

CONTACTING CHURCHES

First, decide which of the thirteen possible ways of identifying available positions are commonly used in your denomination, and also which pertain to your particular goals for ministry. Then contact available churches, keeping in mind the following:

• When writing, keep your letter concise and to the point.

One page is best. Model it as in the sample cover letter shown previously in chapter 4. Convey interest and enthusiasm for the position. Demonstrate your knowledge of it by stating why you believe yourself to be qualified. If you have written previously and are following up on your initial contact, add some new piece of information about yourself and your candidacy, so that you appear to have a logical reason for writing again.

• When phoning, be clear about the purpose of the call and the nature of the information you are seeking.

Are you phoning to express an initial interest in being considered? To find out more about the position? To discover how far along they are in their search? To remind them of your candidacy and gently press for an interview? If necessary, outline in advance the direction you would like the conversation to go. Immediately following the call, jot down highlights of the conversation, including future steps to be taken, and file your notes in the appropriate church folder.

When writing or phoning, if you are planning to be in the area, tell them this, and ask if they would be interested in meeting with you.

Third-Party Contacts

In certain circumstances, it will be to your advantage for a third party to make the initial contact with a church. Such an individual will be perceived as being more objective than you; consequently, their recommendation will tend to carry more weight. Also, if a third party approaches the church on your behalf, the church usually will have an obligation at least to look at you, whereas if your application comes in over the transom, no such obligation exists.

Search your mind for some influential third-party contact—someone who knows you and also knows one or two key laypeople of the church. This individual could be your bishop or judicatory head, your placement officer, a district superintendent, or some influential layperson. Then ask this person whether they would be willing to suggest your name as a possible candidate.

If you are hoping to relocate to another part of the country, you may wish to consider taking a look at the site.

A Personal Visit to the Area

The best time for a visit is during the regular church year, not during vacation season. This way, you can be assured of seeing the people you want to see.

When you are in the area, work your network. Make one contact lead to another. When taking leave of a person, ask, "Who could *you* suggest who might have some leads in the area?" After you return home, write or phone your contacts. Thank them for their assistance. When speaking with prospective churches out of your area, stress that you would be willing to carry all or part of the cost of an interview, or of the move itself. They probably will pick up the cost if you are called, but your offer may open the door to being considered.

GUIDELINES FOR AN EFFECTIVE SEARCH

In this chapter, we have identified thirteen possible ways to discover available positions in the church and to present your name for consideration. In addition, we have described methods of contacting available churches. We now turn to a consideration of guidelines for an effective search. One or two have been mentioned previously, but they bear repeating as you prepare to begin the active phase of your search process.

Form a support group.

Seeking a new call is spiritually and emotionally demanding. You need a supportive group to cheer you on, sympathize with your setbacks, and applaud your triumphs.

At the very minimum, your support group needs to consist of your spouse, perhaps a trusted friend or colleague, and your denominational placement officer. Clergy who have a greater need for emotional support may wish to assemble a highly intentional group, organized for the express purpose of assisting with your search, or you may wish to consider joining an already existing support group. Your nearest clergy career and counseling center (see appendix D) can tell you whether there is a group of job-seeking clergy already meeting in your area.

One technique I highly recommend, and which I have already mentioned, is what author Barbara Sher calls the Buddy System.[4] Following the Buddy System, you meet with another person on a regular basis, to work on mutually set goals. The Buddy System helps keep you focused on the search and guards against procrastination, the enemy of an effective search.

Commit enough scheduled time to your search.

It is estimated that two-thirds of all job hunters in the secular world spend less than five hours a week on their search.[5] I would estimate that clergy seeking a new call probably average well under five hours a week.

Clergy seeking a new call need to think of this as a highly demanding part-time job. There are materials to be mailed out, phone calls to be made, correspondence to be answered. No minister with a current active ministry "has the time" to do all this. You must *make* the time.

This usually means *scheduling* time on a regular basis, to be used only for the search. As mentioned previously, you may conclude that, for you, Thursday morning from 10 A.M. to 12 noon will be search time, and this will take precedence over anything else.

Keep several irons in the fire.

If the polity of your denomination allows it, pursue possibilities with more than one church simultaneously. When you are eliminated for consideration by one church, generate another to take its place. The advantage of this is that you will not be emotionally over-invested in any one church, and consequently, will come across as a more confident candidate. Second, if you *are* in conversation with four or five churches simultaneously, the total length of your search will be considerably more reduced than if you were dealing with only one at a time. If you are in a closed system, indicate to your superintendent or executive pastor that your ministry goals match more than one particular kind of church. Your flexibility will thus be perceived as connectional, rather than self-centered.

Remain engaged with your present ministry.

You must remain emotionally involved in your present ministry while you actively seek out opportunities in other churches. This is not an easy balance to maintain. However, your effectiveness as a candidate depends in no small part upon your continued effectiveness where you are.

Members of your support group may be helpful in assisting you with dealing with the emotional ambiguity of remaining engaged with your present ministry at the same time you actively seek out other possibilities.

"Casing" the Church

If you have followed the suggestions outlined in this chapter, and if, in addition, you have a proven record of effective service in ministry, it will not be long before you are entertaining one or more serious inquiries about the possibility of your being called to a new church.

At this point, the common warning about marriage applies equally well to choosing a new church: "Accept in haste; repent in leisure." Many clergy, to their misfortune, have learned following a call the information they should have learned prior to accepting the call. What information do you need in order to make an informed decision? Second, how can you *obtain* this information in an open system, or in a closed system? We will explore these and other issues in the next chapter, as we discuss "casing" the church.

Chapter Six

"CASING" A CHURCH
What You Need to Know—and Why

Be attentive, that you may gain insight.

Proverbs 4:1*b*

Your materials have now been received by one or more prospective churches. Or your credentials have been presented by a judicatory official to one or more congregations that desire consultation about your appointment. They are actively considering you, and you are actively considering them. Shortly you will be faced with a crucial question: To which of these churches do you feel truly called, in expectation of an effective and productive ministry? In order to make an informed decision, you need adequate information about each church. Your next step, therefore is "casing" the church.[1]

Now you need to know *all relevant information* regarding the prospective church. This relevant information includes "hard data," such as church finances and membership statistics, as well as "soft data," such as a history of past leadership and characteristics of the church's "personality." In closed denominational systems, this kind of information is passed orally from pastor to pastor, and also appears in denominational minutes or reports.

This chapter offers a discussion of *sources of information,* as well as *areas of concern.* We will begin with sources of information, describing each in the order in which you are likely to find it, as you and the church explore with increasing seriousness the possibility of a call or appointment.

SOURCES OF INFORMATION

The Church Itself

The prospective church itself is, of course, the prime source of information. Among the materials you may be sent, or that you may subsequently request, are:
■ congregational information form[2]

74

- membership survey
- annual reports (preferably for the past five years)
- financial report for the last fiscal year
- current annual budget
- church by-laws
- membership directory
- worship attendance reports

In reading the materials available from a prospective church, bring to them the same mind-set you would in reading the real-estate ads in the local newspaper. Just as a house listed as a "fixer" may be, in reality, a house on the verge of collapse, so a "mature congregation" may be one with an average age of 70, and a "changing neighborhood" may be one in which the church is increasingly isolated from its community. Therefore, read all congregational materials "between the lines." If there is something you don't understand or that raises a red flag for you, ask for clarification.

In addition, read the materials in a *pro*active, rather than a *re*active, *frame of mind. Just because the profile states that the previous pastor spent 45 percent of his time on hospital calling, realize that this is not necessarily the way you* would need to allocate your time in order to build a viable and growing congregation.

Denominational Office

Your denominational office is your second prime source of information. Check your denomination's directory of churches for published data on total membership, average attendance, church budget, and Sunday-school enrollment. Talk to your bishop, the district superintendent, or the church's search consultant. Ask if your denominational office has available census-related and/or other demographic information on the town or the area in which the church is located.

Your Network

Your network, especially other clergy in the area, can be a valuable source of information. Keep in mind that their impressions of the church may be highly subjective and will need to be checked against other information. This is especially true of a closed system, where clergy may tend to rely on local gossip, more than on data.

The Local Library

Your local library possesses a wealth of information about any area of the country to which you may consider relocating. For issues relating to the quality of life in your projected area, consult the latest edition of the *Places Rated Almanac,* available in the Reference section.[3] For a corporate spouse concerned about employment opportunities in the new area, the *Rand McNally Commercial Atlas and Marketing Guide,* also in Reference, is published annually and lists pertinent economic and commercial information on major metropolitan areas. Finally, if the town to which you are thinking of relocating is in your own state, your library may subscribe to the local newspaper.

Church Consultants

If you are very serious about a position in a region that is unfamiliar, and you can afford the sizable fee (which could be more than $150), several church consultants have packaged demographic census information about communities, for use by congregations and church leaders. For example, the Presbyterian Church USA supplies this material to Presbyterian congregations (though not for individuals) from their headquarters in Louisville, Kentucky, through the office of New Church Development. Another organization, Percept, in Costa Mesa, California, packages such information, for a fee, to religious professionals. This data might help a pastor develop a scenario (or reveal a concern) for the present and future possibilities in a particular congregation.

Town and Municipal Agencies

More detailed information about an area, including demographics, characteristics of the workforce, and cultural and recreational opportunities, is available from the local Chamber of Commerce, the Tourist Bureau, and the Board of Realtors. For still more detailed information, contact the local Office of Economic Development, and also the

Planning Commission. Allow for a certain amount of "hype," depending upon the source of information.

Previous Pastor

The previous pastor is a prime source of information about the church and the community, and should be contacted, especially when your candidacy advances to the final stages. Sometimes general questions elicit the most useful information.

Ask, for example, "What can you tell me about the congregation?" and see how the person begins their remarks. The present interim (if there is one) can be helpful in viewing the church with a degree of objectivity.

Personal Visit

There is no substitute for a personal visit to the community. Arrive anonymously, if possible, and spend a day, or even half a day, doing a little independent sleuthing. Check out the location of the church and its immediate neighborhood, taking special note of the physical condition of the church buildings. Go downtown and scan the shops. Is this a Big-Mac, or a wine-and-Brie kind of town, or something in between? Check out the real estate listings at a local real-estate office. This will tell you something about the kind of people who are likely to move into the community. If you have time, talk to some local clergy. Then go home and let your impressions "sift" for a few days.

Church Treasurer

When your candidacy reaches its final stages, the treasurer will, of course, be your source of financial information about the church. The kinds of concerns you should bring this individual are discussed under "Church Finances" later in this chapter.

In a closed system, such information might be available from conference reports.

Search Committee

The search committee itself probably is your prime source of information. Your candidating interview is an opportunity to explore issues raised in your own mind by the printed materials you have been sent, as well as by your general impressions of the church and the community. Remember, the interview is your chance to *ask* questions as well as *be* asked. Questions for a candidate to ask, designed to elicit necessary information about the church, are explored in chapter 7.

WHAT YOU NEED TO KNOW

So far in this chapter, we have discussed *sources* of information about a prospective church. We turn now to the information itself that you need in order to make an informed decision about the church.

Church Finances: General Purposes Budget

Is the budget in excess of $100,000? If it is *not,* you will probably be squeezed in terms of salary increases and programmatic expansion, to say nothing of basic maintenance of the buildings. (The base line figure of $100,000 will vary from $75,000 to $130,000, depending upon the cost of living in the area of the country in which the church is located.)

If the church budget is considerably *under* $100,000, and your plan is to raise it to a more adequate level during your first few years at the church, be realistic about what this would involve. Better yet, think through a form of planned change that might be necessary for this particular church. A church with a current budget of $80,000 would need to be increased 13 percent a year, in order to reach your target level of the equivalent of $100,000 at the end of three years, figuring inflation at 5 percent a year. Ask yourself: Are there prospects for growth in the community? And also, do you have proven gifts for evangelism or for the processes of high-quality ministry that would tend to support such expectations?

Look next at the proportion of the budget allocated for staff salaries and benefits, and also for programs. Staff salaries and benefits should not exceed 50 to 60 percent of the total church budget. If they constitute two-thirds or more of the budget, the labor costs are too high, and the church is financially stretched. If the pastor's compensation alone, including cash salary, housing costs, and utilities, is *more* than 30 percent of the budget, and if the program budget is *under* 15 to 20 percent, it is further evidence that the church is financially pinched.

Check for accuracy and for evidence of good stewardship in church financial reporting. Beware of rounded-off figures, unexplained zigs and zags in income from one year to the next, and declining revenues. If the church's annual report shows evidence of any of these, you want an explanation before you agree to come.

In discussing finances with church officials, beware of poor-mouthing attitudes, or of claims that the church is, in some way, unique among churches of the denomination in terms of its finances. Such assertions may be a smoke screen to cover shoddy financial planning or to discourage reasonable salary expectations on the part of the pastor. You may be called to help them sort out these matters, but you should also think introspectively about whether you have the training and gifts of a change agent.

Sources of Income

Look at the amount pledged as a proportion of the total operating budget. If it is *under* 60 percent, members are not carrying their own weight and are relying on other sources of income (i.e., endowments).

Now look at nonpledge income. If it is in excess of 20 to 25 percent of the budget, are these sources of income reliable? Is a large proportion of it from a single rental lease that is shortly due to expire, for example? Is there a large annual gift from a single source, or are certain sources of income restricted?

Some pastors take a cue from business leaders who believe that an organization or church can be revitalized, or better, be able to maintain an innovative edge, if it is willing to spend down excessive capital reserves (but not all funds for a rainy day), so that they depend more on the life within the present body, and less on the monuments to the past. When "casing" a church, you will want to know how the church perceives its reserves.

Debt

Church debt comes chiefly in the form of mortgages on church properties and outstanding loans for recent building improvements and renovations.

Ten to 15 percent indebtedness as a proportion of the total budget is normative. However, if it is over 25 percent, it will tend to limit programmatic expansion, place a cap on staff salaries, and involve the pastor in extensive fund-raising activities. Your ministry objectives might not match these circumstances.

Look also to see how any outstanding loans are structured. For example, if there is a balloon payment due in the near future (ask the treasurer), the church's present financial picture will change dramatically, and you need to know.

Giving Per Member

How does the giving per member compare with the average in your denomination? If it is significantly higher than usual, or if it is lower, then you have cause for elation or for concern, respectively. (Giving will skew lower than average for an inner-city or blue-collar congregation, and higher than average for a suburban congregation.) The number of giving units should be about 60 percent of the total congregational membership. If the total number is under 50 percent, then either membership rolls are padded or stewardship is not taken seriously. Ask how pledge drives are conducted. Usually, the more personal (i.e., actual calling on members) the better, and the more seriously stewardship is taken.

Clergy Compensation

Finding out what the church is prepared to pay a new pastor can be surprisingly difficult. If the church publishes a salary range for the position, you are relieved of further stress or doubt. If not, request annual reports for one to two years back, and look up your predecessor's salary. Keep in mind the fact that what the previous pastor was making is not necessarily the figure the church is prepared to offer a new person.

If you *are* able to obtain a reasonable idea of the salary and benefits the church is prepared to offer (this would include cash salary, housing allowance, utilities, and any other item that contributes materially to the dollars you would actually receive), compare these figures with comparable figures for your present position. Calculate any possible cost-of-living difference between your present area and the one in which the church is located (don't rely on the prospective church's estimate of this; talk to an objective third party), and you will be able to estimate whether you and your family would be better off financially in this new position.

In order to determine how much room there is for negotiating salary and benefits, compare the salary range they list, or the compensation paid the previous pastor, with *the average compensation for a similar position in your denomination.* Talk to your placement officer for this information. Keep in mind that blue-collar and inner-city congregations tend to skew lower in salary in relation to the total church budget, and wealthy churches and suburban churches tend to skew higher. The difference between what the church is prepared to offer and the average compensation for a similar position is your room to negotiate.

For a more detailed discussion of negotiating salary and benefits, see the next chapter.

In considering housing, you will naturally look at the quality and condition of the parsonage. If you would prefer a housing *allowance,* so that you could rent or purchase your own home, you need to explore the possibility of this with the church. Housing matters are discussed in more detail in the next chapter.

Church Attendance

Church attendance is probably the most accurate indication of the true size of a congregation. If the average Sunday attendance during the main church year (September through May) is less than 25 percent of total reported membership, then membership figures are padded, or there are problems in the congregation. In a small church, look for 50 percent of the members to be attending on an average Sunday. In a large church, the proportion of members attending will tend to be lower, nearer 33 percent. In independent or nondenominational congregations, membership is conceived or accounted differently, so that worship attendance is probably the only accountable or reported figure.

Congregational Demographics

Refer to the church profile for a breakdown of congregational members' occupational and educational characteristics. Investigate also the community in which the church is located. Remember that Episcopal, Unitarian, and Presbyterian congregations will tend to skew higher on the socioeconomic scale than the community as a whole.

Once you have determined the predominant socioeconomic background of the congregation, ask yourself what this means, in terms of your intended ministry and also your preferred leadership style. In general, working-class and blue-collar congregations prefer a pastor with a more directive leadership style.[4] Professional and managerial congregations, however, prefer a more collegial, participating style, but such congregations also can be highly demanding in terms of the quality of services they expect from the church.

Try to determine also the average age of congregational members. This will have implications not only in terms of programming, but also as an indication of congregational growth or decline. Look to the proportion of weddings and baptisms, indicating a younger membership, as opposed to burials, indicating an aging membership. Also, look to church school attendance figures. Church growth experts believe that the Sunday school is a bellwether of future church growth or decline. Has church school enrollment been increasing or decreasing in recent years? Also, what is the percentage of church school *attendance* to church school *enrollment?* It should be about 60 percent. If it is under 50 percent, you will have to strengthen the church school.

Finally, what is the proportion of old to new members? If long-term members comprise more than a quarter of the congregation, historical pressures are likely to be heavy on the new pastor. If, on the other hand, a majority of the people are recent members, there probably will be an openness to new ideas, but there also may be a need to span a gulf between the old and the new members.

The Community

Find out all you can about the community. If you and your family will not be happy in the community, it is likely that you also will not be happy in the church.

What is the nature of the community? Is it small-town mid-America, inner city, blue collar, suburban, academic, or something else? Do you feel called to work in this environment? Would your family feel comfortable living here?

If the church expresses a desire to grow, are there realistic prospects for this in the community? Look at where existing members live, in relation to the church. If more than 15 percent drive in from outlying areas (10 to 15 miles or more), then you have a commuting church, and long-range prospects for growth are not good.

If you have children, investigate area schools. Are the teachers experienced and qualified? How large are the classes? What are the combined math and verbal SAT scores of students in the local high school? (A score of 1,000 or more is good.) How many graduates go on to college? Seventy-five percent is the sign of a top quality school. In the more affluent suburbs, 90 percent or more will go on.

Previous Pastor

What were the circumstances of the previous pastor's leaving? Did they retire or resign, or were they terminated? If they were fired, this is definitely something you want to know before you accept the call.

How *long* have previous pastors stayed, and what does this seem to say about the church? In *open* systems, a history of short-term pastorates may suggest a lack of verve in the church, poor remuneration, or an inflexible and entrenched *lay* power structure. In a *closed* system, a history of short-term pastorates (less than 2 or 3 years) may suggest a lack of verve in the church or district, poor remuneration, or an inflexible and entrenched *clergy* power structure.) A previous long-term pastorate, however, may also prove difficult to follow. In such a case, the use of an interim appointment is highly recommended.

Was the previous pastor liked or disliked? If they were liked, the church will be looking for someone who is similar. If they were disliked, the church will be looking for someone who is *opposite*. They also will be looking for strengths in areas where the last person was weak.

What *were* the strengths and weaknesses of your predecessor? Churches will seek to duplicate the previous pastor's strengths, but *they will tend to take them for granted in the successor.* Therefore, find out what these areas of strengths were, so you can judge whether or not you possess them.

Finally, if your predecessor lives in the community, what is their relation with their former church? Do they expect to be involved, and if so, how? If possible, meet your predecessor during candidating week and decide such matters as who will do the funeral of a longtime member if that occurs two weeks after you arrive.

Church "Personality"

Kent R. Hunter, in *Your Church Has Personality,* states that every church has a personality.[5] This personality affects the way the church sees itself and how it conceives and carries out its mission. John David Webb, in *How to Change the Image of Your Church,* puts the same idea in terms of communications theory.[6] It is similar to what, in a business context, might be called the "corporate culture," or "company image." This personality probably will not be expressed in so many words by church members. It must be intuited—by you. And if you accept the call, it will be embodied within you.

Ask yourself some basic questions of the church: What is its sense of vocation or mission? What does it get excited about? Where does it "invest" its time, talent, and treasure? Who does it primarily minister *to?* What is its preferred style of pastoral leadership? To get at the answers to some of these concerns, ask a playful question: If this church were an animal, would it be: (a) a guard dog, getting ready to attack; (b) a regal lion, yawning and stretching in the sun; or (c) a friendly puppy, bouncing up for a hug?

When you believe you have a sense of the church's personality, ask yourself whether your style of ministry would seem to be "in sync" with the expectations of a majority of the members.

Congregational Goals

Somewhere in the materials the church has sent you, you should find a section that describes congregational goals for the future. In order to gauge the level of congregational support for the stated goals, check to see whether at least half the congregation participated in the survey. (If it was less than a third, the results may be skewed.) In general, the goals a congregation states for itself should be taken seriously. If your interests lie in other areas, you should consider a call to another church.

Church Staff

In larger churches, the paid staff already in place when you arrive is probably the largest potential source of conflict during that crucial first year of ministry.[7]

While candidating, try to meet with individual members of the paid staff to get a sense of how they conceive their roles. Does anybody on the staff operate his or her particular fiefdom? Is anybody on the staff, in reality, unable to be fired (like that 20-year organist, for example)? If you are offered the call, consider conducting a staff retreat, with an outside facilitator, at the earliest opportunity.

Power Structure

Where does the real power in the congregation lie? What group (either formally or informally constituted) actually runs the church? *Is* it the central governing body, or is there another group or committee that vies for power? Who are the key individuals or groups in the church that would need to be consulted on any major decision? What are the congregational "limits," both in terms of minimal pastoral duties that *must* be performed, and also in terms of transgressions that cannot be tolerated? (Ask the search committee, during candidating week, what would be the quickest way for the new pastor to get into trouble around here?)

If the church's style of governance is strongly congregational, peruse the sections that pertain to you. Who hires and fires the minister? What are the procedures involved? What are your rights (i.e., control of worship) and limitations (i.e., approval of use of the buildings)? Above all, if you see anything in the bylaws that would affect your accepting a call to the church, bring this matter before the search committee and have it resolved to your satisfaction before you accept the call.

Weighing a Call

You have "cased" the church. Now you must decide, on the basis of available evidence, whether this is the church to which God is calling you. Some of us who rely more on relationships and intuition to make decisions will not have perused the data above with as much rigor as those who rely on analytical ability to make quick or firm judgments.

Beware the Halo Effect

The Halo Effect is the tendency to see any church as you want it to be, either in terms of being *better* than it really is, or in terms of possessing the particular *characteristics* you are looking for. The Halo Effect will increase in direct proportion to your eagerness—or your desperation—to get a new call.

Another characteristic of the Halo Effect is the tendency to believe that, if you came, you would be able to transform this church into your ideal image of ministry.

Watch out! Matches between a church and a pastor based upon the expectations of changing either for the better are probably about as successful as marriages based upon similar expectations. All things being equal, it is safest to draw this conclusion:

• This church I see in front of me is what it is. Furthermore, it is probably happy remaining what it is. The church I see is the church I will get.

If what you see in not congruent with your vision for ministry, then probably the fairest course for both you and the church is to pursue your vision elsewhere.

If you are absolutely convinced, however, that this place has the *potential* to become what you envision, ask yourself some tough-minded questions:

• Exactly what needs to happen in this situation in order to transform it?

• Do I have the particular skills and abilities needed to make that occur?

And, finally, most important:

• Is there hard evidence that what I want and what they want are one and the same?

If you are realistic, you will realize that the church you finally accept will inevitably be a compromise between your ideal vision and what exists in reality.

How Much Should I Compromise?

Ultimately, only you can answer that. Furthermore, the answer will depend upon how long you have been in the search process and how eager you are to get a new position. However, in order not to be unduly swayed by either the Halo Effect on the one hand, or desperation and panic on the other, it would be wise to:
• Review periodically your ministry objectives.
• Accept a new call only if most of your ministry objectives would be met.

I do not mean to suggest that if the church has some real problems, you should cross it off your list. Some very gifted clergy are called to a ministry of resurrecting troubled churches. I *am* saying, however, that you need to be realistic about the nature of the situation you are committing to, and, in the words of scripture, "count the cost" before you take the next step.

The Next Step

It has happened! They have "cased" you, you have "cased" them, and a member of the search committee is on the phone, asking whether you could come for an interview two weeks from Thursday. Your heart is racing with a mixture of excitement and apprehension. We turn now to the next step in the search process—the candidating interview.

Chapter Seven

THE CANDIDATING INTERVIEW

Do not worry about how you are to speak or what you are to say.

Matthew 10:19

I'll never forget my first interview with a church search committee. The committee was not clear about its purpose, and consequently I kept asking myself, What is the real purpose of this interview? What do they want to hear from me? What do I want to hear from them? How could this interview help both of us discover whether God is calling us into closer association?

These and other questions, as well as practical concerns regarding the interview, are discussed in this chapter. For pastors in a closed or connectional system, the interview may occur in a more informal process, or it may take place further upstream, but the same strategies are at work in discerning God's will.

MUTUAL EXPLORATION

The most important thing to say about the interview is that it is, or should be, a process of *mutual* exploration, whereby you and a church explore together whether God is calling you into a closer association. To do this, you present yourself as a *resource person*. You explore with them—and they with you—whether *your* gifts and *their* needs are mutually complementary.

What Churches Are Looking For

Obviously, churches are looking for a variety of qualities in their spiritual leader, but they certainly would include most of the following:

- energy and enthusiasm
- faith and spiritual depth
- proven qualities of leadership
- effectiveness in preaching
- pastoral empathy and administrative competence
- ability to minister to *all* members

- willingness to commit to the congregation's goals for the future
- proven record of effectiveness in ministry.

The One Big Question

The one big question on the minds of search committee members is, If we call this person, what will be the style and pattern of ministry? What kind of leadership have they exercised in the past, and what kind are they therefore likely to exercise in the future? The same questions occur in the minds of executives who consult with pastors in a closed system. The candidates who can intuit these unspoken questions in the minds of search committee members, and can respond clearly to them, have done *them* a service, and may be well on the way to receiving a new call.

PREPARING FOR THE INTERVIEW

When the search committee phones to schedule an interview, you need to achieve clarification on several matters:

• When do they want to schedule a visit? If you are one of several candidates, it will be to your advantage to be seen toward the end.

• Who will be making travel arrangements for you? What is this person's name?

• How are finances being handled? Do they agree to reimburse you for travel related expenses?

• What is the charge of the committee? Is it *this committee* that will make the final selection?

• What is the schedule for your visit? Will the committee allow time for *your* questions, and also some "down" time for you and your family?

• What is the nature of your accommodations? Will you be put up in paid accommodations, or in the home of a church member? (If the latter, just remember that you will be "on" for the duration of your visit.)

• Will they want you to preach and/or conduct a service?

After the call, write down the essence of the conversation and follow up with a letter, confirming your understanding of the arrangements.

Review All Materials

Read over the materials that are available concerning this church. Ask yourself, What problems and challenges does this church have that I could help them solve? Pay particular attention to their top three goals for ministry.

Review your own placement materials. Pay particular attention to the pastoral specialties you listed, and also to your section on pastoral leadership style. These probably will be a source of some of their questions to you.

Review in your own mind questions you are likely to be asked, and also questions you want to ask them. (Examples are discussed in detail later in this chapter.) You also may want to prepare by reviewing some books on effective interviewing.[1]

Prepare Your Sermon

If you are to preach, prepare a sermon that is a particularly effective version of your characteristic style and content. Do not attempt to preach in a style or method that is not fully yours. You will only be setting yourself up for expectations that you cannot fulfill, should you be called. Remember the qualities of a good sermon—brief and to the point, with a clearly defined topic, supported by real-life examples of faith at work. If you are able to preach without notes, so much the better.

How to Dress

In general, err on the side of formality. (This applies to your spouse as well.) Remember, as John Malloy and others have pointed out,[2] darker colors tend to invest the person wearing them with a sense of authority. Darker colors are especially advantageous for physically small individuals, and also for female clergy.

Mental Attitude

Remind yourself that the search committee would not be calling you if they were not already favorably impressed with you. Remind yourself also that, of all the people in the room, you probably will be the most knowledgeable about church affairs. Your task is to communicate clearly and effectively what you already know, and, of course, relate it to the needs and concerns of this particular church.

THE INTERVIEW

Research has shown that people gain their first impression of others within seven seconds of meeting them.[3] Therefore, your first moments with a search committee will be crucial in forming their first impression of you. When you first meet them, extend a firm handshake and establish eye contact with each member. As the interview progresses, avoid annoying personal mannerisms, such as slouching, fidgeting, or mumbling. Answer questions clearly and concisely, be courteous and tactful, and, in general, demonstrate "maturity" by the appropriateness of your responses and your sensitivity to each questioner. In preparation for the interview, keep in mind the following six rules for effective candidating.

Six Rules for Candidating

> **1. Start strong.**

Crucial interview questions, such as, "Why do you feel called to this church?" often come early in the interview. You therefore need to be prepared to "jump right in" the moment the interview begins.

> **2. Listen carefully.**

Hear what the members of the committee are saying, as well as what they may *not* be saying! Listen for nuances. Observe interaction among various individuals. (The presence of your spouse may be very helpful in noting dynamics of the interview you may have missed.) Notice significant reactions (glances, silence) on the part of committee members to statements you or others have made. During the course of the interview, ask for clarification if needed: What do you mean by that? Could you give me an example?

> **3. Maintain a balance between listening and talking.**

Studies of successful applicants have shown that individuals who do well in an interview tend to mix listening and talking about 50-50. Try to avoid speaking continuously for more than two minutes at any one time.

> **4. Avoid being drawn into controversial issues.**

If you are asked your opinion on current controversial issues, simply state your position clearly and succinctly, and allow the interview to move on. Do not get trapped into a debate with your questioner.

> **5. Convey enthusiasm about the prospect of being called.**

While the interview is a *mutual* exploration, as stated previously, the members of the search committee still want to hear that you are excited about the prospect of being called.

> **6. Answer questions in a clear and succinct manner, with *specific references* to your previous ministry, and to the stated needs of the prospective church.**

One of the best ways of formulating answers to specific questions is to use what is called the T-BAR Technique:[4]

T-BAR Technique

The T-BAR Technique takes its name from a four-step process of responding to questions:

Topic sentence
Background
Action
Results

Suppose, for example, you are asked how you support lay ministry. You might respond in the following manner:

■ **Topic Sentence**

I've always been highly supportive of lay ministry. One example that comes to mind is . . .

■ **Background**

When I first came to my present church, I kept hearing that the same people were always being called on to do everything, and a lot of them were feeling burned out.

■ **Action**

I decided to find out why more people were not volunteering. I distributed a questionnaire to all the members. I discovered that a majority of them felt they lacked the training to accept major leadership positions. Consequently, I presented to the Board of Deacons a proposal that the church institute a program of leadership training for lay people.

■ **Results**

During the past five years, more than thirty people have gone through this training program, and we have more than doubled the number of people currently involved in major leadership roles in the church.

The advantage of the T-BAR Technique, as illustrated above, is that it helps to keep your answers clear and focused as you relate previous accomplishments to the needs of the church for which you are candidating.

Typical Questions

The following are some typically asked questions of candidates seeking a new position:

Could you tell us something about yourself?

What they are trying to find out: An ice-breaker, this question is designed to gain a sense of you as an individual, and also what is most real to you about your ministry.

How to respond: Give a brief biography, emphasizing the aspects that relate most directly to the needs of the church for which you are candidating.

What is it about our church that appeals to you?

What they are trying to find out: Whether you have taken the trouble to read their materials, and also whether your personal ministry goals are consistent with the needs of the church.

How to respond: Describe your attraction to the position in terms of the congregation's stated goals for ministry. Be willing to communicate enthusiasm at the prospect of being called.

Why do you want to leave your present position?

What they are trying to find out: Whether your desire to move is part of a natural career progression, or whether you are in trouble.

How to respond: If your move is a natural career progression, say that you believe you have accomplished the essence of what you set out to do in your present position (describe some recent accomplishments), and you feel it is now time to move on to greater challenges in ministry. If, however, you are under pressure to resign or have even been terminated from your present position, turn to the section on "Terminated Clergy" in chapter 10 for some suggestions about how to respond.

What do you consider to be your major strengths and weaknesses? What have been your greatest accomplishments?

What they are trying to find out: Whether your gifts are consistent with the needs of the church, whether you are secure enough to admit to weaknesses, and whether your weaknesses would, in any way, be a serious detriment to the future ministry of the church.

How to respond: Be honest about your strengths. If these are not what the church needs, you and they need to know this now, before you attempt to carry out ministry together. If your strengths do match the needs of the church, and hopefully this will be the case, make your presentation clearly and persuasively, using statistics ("stewardship has increased 50 percent over the past 5 years") and well-chosen anecdotes to make your case.

Responding to the question about weaknesses gives you an opportunity to state candidly which areas of ministry are of less interest to you. Be prepared to explain, however, how you would address these areas—through the use of lay ministry, for example.

How would you describe your leadership style?

What they are trying to find out: Whether your leadership style fits church norms and expectations, and also whether your style invites lay people into participation.

How to respond: Be honest. If you believe that the senior pastor is the one who initiates major leadership decisions, now is the time to say so.

However, be sure to communicate a sense that you invite the church membership into active participation in all leadership decisions. Give search committee members an example of your leadership style, using the T-BAR Technique to demonstrate how a recent decision in your church was reached. (Special issues relating to the leadership style of female clergy are discussed in chapter 10.)

Could you describe a conflict situation in your ministry, and how you handled it?

What they are trying to find out: Whether you are honest enough to admit that you have faced conflict, and also whether you have the emotional maturity to handle it in a creative and forthright manner, to the benefit of all parties.

How to respond: Don't say that you have never faced a conflict. Instead, describe a conflict situation where action needed to be taken for the greater good of the whole church. Describe your role in resolving the conflict; tell what you learned about yourself and about your leadership style from the manner in which you resolved it.

What is your position on women's ordination, abortion, the ordination of homosexuals, liturgical renewal, the church's involvement in politics, divorce, or other controversial issues?

What they are trying to find out: Whether your theological and political orientation is within the range of acceptability for their church.

How to respond: Avoid being drawn into a lengthy debate. Simply state your position on a particular issue clearly and forthrightly. If you have not made up your mind on a particular issue, say that you are still waiting for God's guidance. If your questioner seems to want to draw you into a lengthy debate, say that you will be glad to discuss the issue at greater length after the interview.

Is there anything else we should know about you?

What they are trying to find out: Whether you have major strengths or weaknesses on which the committee has not yet touched.

How to respond: This question provides the opportunity to bring up special qualifications or interests that have not been discussed. If the interview never touched on that program of home Bible study which you initiated, now is the time to bring it up.

Now is also the time to raise issues of a potentially problematic or limiting nature related to your candidacy. If, for example, you have been terminated from your present church, turn to chapter 10 for suggestions about how to respond to this during the interview.

Would you accept this position if it were offered to you?

What they are trying to find out: Whether you share a sense of excitement at the prospect of ministry together.

How to respond: You need to communicate a genuine sense of excitement and enthusiasm at the prospect of being called, at the same time affirming that it is the Holy Spirit who will make the final decision about whether you are called to work together.

YOUR QUESTIONS

Some church placement professionals suggest that as much as half the interview time be allocated for the candidate's questions and concerns. The purpose is to corroborate, clarify, and supplement your knowledge of the church, so that you can make an informed decision as to whether or not you are called. Among the questions you may consider asking are the following:

What do you consider the most pressing needs and concerns facing this congregation now and in the future?

What you are trying to find out: What are the issues that would set your agenda for the immediate future? Do you personally have an interest—or an expertise—in dealing with these particular issues?

If a new family moves to the community, why might they be attracted to the church? What might tend to keep them away?

What you are trying to find out: What is the self-image of this congregation? What do they feel proud about? What organizations in the congregation are most active? Conversely, what areas of congregational life have been neglected, and what impediments to growth exist in the congregation?

What were the greatest strengths of the previous pastor? In what areas could they perhaps have been stronger?

What you are trying to find out: In what areas of ministry will there be a pent-up demand (your predecessor's weaknesses), and in what other areas will pastoral competence be assumed (your predecessor's strengths)?

Why are you interested in me as a candidate for this position?

What you are trying to find out: What is their perception of your strengths? Are they reading you accurately? Is their perception of your strengths consistent with your own understanding of your gifts and abilities?

What would be the fastest way for the pastor to get into trouble around here?

What you are trying to find out: What are the norms of congregational life that cannot be violated, except at the minister's own peril?

How has the minister's family traditionally been involved in the church?

What you are trying to find out: What are the expectations of your spouse and family? Are their expectations consistent with your family's patterns of involvement in the past?

How is the minister's compensation arrived at, and by whom?

What you are trying to find out: What are the actual procedures by which the minister's compensation is determined? Is the minister involved in the process?

In general, what is the church's attitude toward providing adequate clergy compensation? (Salary issues will be discussed at greater length in the next chapter.)

If you could give one piece of advice to the new minister, what would it be?

What you are trying to find out: A kind of summary question, you are inviting the committee to express any last thoughts or feelings about the challenges of the position. On a subliminal level, you are also inviting the committee to participate in your potential new ministry in the church.

In addition to the questions above, if you have special concerns to bring before the search committee, such as what housing options are available to you (see "Clergy Housing Concerns" in chapter 9), a portion of the interview should be used to address such concerns.

"THE CLOSE"

Any salesperson will tell you that "The Close" is the most important part of a sale. This is the point where the salesperson builds on all that has been said, then moves the client to a decision. When you sense the interview winding down, or when the chair indicates that it is concluding, you may summarize what you have heard during the interview. Begin by thanking the committee for considering you for the position. Review some highlights of the interview, summarizing your qualifications for the position, and conclude by saying that the Holy Spirit will now direct both you and the church in making the right decision.

The Clergy Spouse

The clergy spouse has an important role to play in the candidating process. The spouse is in an excellent position to act as the candidate's eyes and ears, observing the dynamics of the interview and of the process in general, and afterward, sharing impressions. In addition, from the church's point of view, the search committee has a legitimate need to gain a sense of the spouse's style and personality, and how such characteristics might affect the candidate's ministry.

If the spouse is asked how they intend to be involved in the life of the church, their best answer is to describe how they have been involved in the past, and indicate that the pattern is likely to continue in the future, unless, of course, major life changes occur in the meantime.

THE TOUGH OR DYSFUNCTIONAL COMMITTEE

Unfortunately, not all interviews are conducted by committees with a clear or appropriate sense of their charge. Clergy occasionally will encounter a tough or a dysfunctional committee. You will recognize the tough committee by the fact that members tend to ask "stress" questions and, in general, treat you as a hired hand. The dysfunctional committee, on the other hand, seems not to have its act together, and often evidences strange dynamics within the committee itself.

Your role with the tough committee is to assert yourself in such a way that you become an equal partner in the relationship. Your role with the dysfunctional committee is to assume the necessary degree of leadership, in order to make the interview "work." With both, you will need to ask yourself: If the people in the committee represent the leadership of the church, what are the implications of this for me in terms of my future ministry?

Your Right to Privacy

The characteristics of the tough committee, but also of an increasing number of search processes in general, is that they may request your permission to investigate sensitive personal matters, such as any evidence of sexual impropriety in your past, and possibly even your financial and credit history. This grows out of the church's understandable desire to uncover any possible areas of sexual or financial difficulties. However, it also poses a question for you as a candidate:

What is your legitimate right to privacy, and how far will you go in supplying personal information to a search committee?

If in doubt, contact your denominational office and find out what kinds of queries are considered appropriate. It may be that particular questions or a request for particular kinds of information are now considered generally acceptable within your denomination. However, if you discover that the committee's intended lines of inquiry do indeed go beyond accepted bounds, then you, as the candidate, must decide whether to comply with their request, even at the risk of possibly being eliminated from consideration for the position.

Staff Position

The interview for an assistant's position is simpler than that for senior pastor, in that you most likely will be interviewing with one individual—the senior pastor—rather than with a committee. The major issue for you is to determine what it would be like to work for this person. You may want to do some reference checking of your own, contacting predecessors in this position and asking about their experience working for this individual.

During the interview with the senior pastor, you need to find out what areas of responsibilities you would be assigned, and you need to indicate areas of ministry in which you feel you have unusual strengths.

FOLLOW UP

Shortly after you return home from the interview, write down your impressions. The following checklist may prove helpful:[5]

AFTER INTERVIEW CHECKLIST

For what position: _____ Date: _____
Where it took place: _____
Advance arrangements for travel and accommodations were
    satisfactorily planned: _____ fulfilled: _____
Advance documentation:
    My own: I was satisfied ____ They were satisfied ____
    Theirs: I was satisfied ____ They were satisfied ____

My own personal appearance (dress, grooming, etc.)
    was appropriate for the occasion: _____
Initial meeting with interviewers (on arrival): Comments:
Initial meeting with others (spouses, other clergy,
    secretary, sexton, organist, etc.):
My opening statements in interview—Comments:
Their opening statements in interview—Comments:
Their questions which I handled well:
Their questions which I wish I had handled better:
My questions which were answered to my satisfaction:
My questions which were not answered to my satisfaction:
Further exchange of information
    What I expect from them
    What they expect from me
Time-table to decision
How I feel about the position after this interview
How well do I like the people; the challenge
Arrangements, if any, for discussion with Bishop (or
    equivalent judicatory head)
Names of key people and personal notes
People I should contact when I get home

Share your impressions with your support group. Tell them what excited you about the church, but also what puzzled or disturbed you during the interview, and ask for their insights.

After the interview, guard against the tendency to be overly critical of yourself or of your performance. Keep in mind that you cannot "sell" yourself to a church if it is not the will of the Holy Spirit that you be called.

Thank-You Letters

Shortly after you return home, write thank-you letters to all the principles involved in the candidating process. This includes: (1) the chair of the search committee; (2) an overnight host; (3) a luncheon or dinner host; (4) a designated guide to the community; and (5) anybody else who went out of their way to make your visit comfortable and enjoyable.

In addition to demonstrating common courtesy, thank-you notes are a way of reminding key church leaders of your interest in the position, during the period immediately following your visit.

Waiting, Waiting, Waiting . . .

Now comes the tough part—waiting to hear the church's decision. During this time, you need to keep actively involved with your present church, carrying on your ministry, and also, depending upon the polity of your denomination, continuing to contact other prospective churches.

When You Finally Hear

Eventually the search committee will contact you, either to extend a call or to inform you that you are no longer a candidate.

If you *are* being called, ask how long you have to respond. Usually, you will have at least two weeks. This will allow you to get in touch with other churches with whom you may be in contact about the status of your candidacy. This is especially important if there is another church to which you feel more strongly called. If your candidacy is at an early stage in this other church, you have a difficult decision to make.

If, however, a member of the search committee phones to let you know that another candidate has been called, try to ascertain why you were eliminated from consideration. Word your inquiry something like this: "I want to thank you and the committee for considering me. Yours is the type of position I am hoping eventually to obtain. I wonder if you could share with me any ways that I might be able to present myself more effectively for such positions in the future." Whatever information you are able to obtain, apply it to your next candidacy, as seems appropriate.

Accepting a Call

It has finally happened! A church has phoned to say that they are prepared to call you as their next pastor. You are now at a moment of decision. How do you decide whether this call, or perhaps another one, represents God's will for you and your ministry?

A wise pastor once said to me, "When weighing such decisions, listen to your heart." Ask yourself to which of these possibilities do you find yourself drawn? For which do you find yourself making preliminary plans? Which sends you to a map to find out where you would be living? Ask yourself these and similar questions, and most likely the Holy Spirit will lead you to a particular choice.

In addition to listening to your heart, you need also to listen to your head. Go back to chapter 3 of this book. Review your personal ministry goals. Ask yourself, "Are my ministry goals truly consistent with the needs of this particular church?"

Look also at the strength of the congregational mandate you have received. If a congregational vote is required, 90 percent or more constitutes a strong mandate. Eighty percent or less, however, poses a question as to whether you would be wise to accept. If your call is based on a vote of the governing board alone, some pastors insist on a unanimous vote before accepting a new call.

Beware of a tendency to jump at a call—any call—out of fear that it is the only one you will receive. This is especially a temptation to midcareer clergy being offered a call to a significantly larger congregation! Many pastor/church conflicts, and even terminations, have resulted from mismatches made in haste and desperation. Again, listen to your heart as well as your head, and rely on the Holy Spirit to lead you and the church into the right decision for both of you.

Chapter Eight

LETTER OF AGREEMENT

Then the whole assembly made a covenant . . . in the house of God.

II Chronicles 23:3

If you seek placement in an open system, when a church is preparing to call you as their new pastor, you will sign a Letter of Agreement with that church. Called in various denominations a Letter of Calling, Letter of Contract, Clergy Contract, Clergy Covenant, or Letter of Agreement, this document insures that you and the church are in agreement concerning exactly what you expect from each other.

Second, a Letter of Agreement, carefully drafted, will help raise issues that neither you nor the church may have considered at the time of the call, such as who will pay for pulpit supply when you are on vacation, for example. Finally, a Letter of Agreement is a way of insuring that your understandings with the church at the time of the issuing of the call are passed on to each new generation of leaders in the church.

In a closed appointment system, formal and written expectations about clergy performance are initially non-negotiable. Salaries, benefits, and housing expectations are published and therefore are non-ssues when the pastor agrees to serve. Later, many of these issues of performance and reward evolve within a committee that works on pastor/parish relations. Many of the strategies named below will still apply to the ongoing process of negotiating and rewarding clergy performance.

A Letter of Agreement consists of three major parts, although these three parts may not be clearly differentiated in the actual document:

- Position Description
  Your duties and (possibly) goals to be achieved.
- Salary and Benefits
  Cash stipend, housing, and all other benefits.
- Ministry Review
  Guidelines for periodic evaluations.

In this chapter we will discuss the specific provisions contained in a Letter of Agreement in some detail. For particulars as to how your own

103

Letter of Agreement should be written, consult the appropriate staff person at your denominational office.

We will begin our discussion by describing the information you need in order to negotiate a satisfactory Letter of Agreement.

INFORMATION YOU NEED

- Your present compensation, including salary and benefits
  Use the following chart as a guide for listing your present compensation.[1] In this way you can make a meaningful comparison between what you are now earning and what the new church is prepared to offer you.
- A copy of the Letter of Agreement recommended by your denominational office
  Note any differences between the form the church plans to use and the form suggested by your denominational office.
- Compensational guidelines from your denominational office
  As a supplement to these, you may also wish to consult additional resources on the subject of clergy compensation.[2]
- Church Annual Report (if possible)
  Note especially the church's *total annual budget* and your *predecessor's salary.*

THE COST OF A PROFESSIONAL MINISTRY

	What I Have	What They Offer	What I Want
1. Professional expense reimbursements			
a. Automobile: all costs	_____	_____	_____
b. Continuing ed. costs	_____	_____	_____
c. Prof. books, etc.	_____	_____	_____
d. Discretionary funds	_____	_____	_____
Total prof. expenses	_____	_____	_____
2. Supplemental benefits			
a. Pension plan	_____	_____	_____
b. Death benefit plan	_____	_____	_____

c. Health benefits plan
   (Family coverage)   _____   _____   _____
d. Dental care plan
   (Family coverage)   _____   _____   _____
e. Medical exp.
   reimbursements   _____   _____   _____
f. Malpractice insurance   _____   _____   _____
g. Key person life ins.   _____   _____   _____
   Total supplemental benefits _____   _____   _____
3. Housing
   a. Housing allowance   _____   _____   _____
   b. Parsonage costs   _____   _____   _____
   c. Utilities allowance   _____   _____   _____
   d. Furnishings allowance _____   _____   _____
   e. Housing equity allowance _____   _____   _____
4. Cash salary   _____   _____   _____

Total Cost   _____   _____   _____

In addition to the preceding information, you also will want to know the charge of the committee with whom you will be meeting. Are they the ones who are empowered to ratify the agreement, or must it be approved by another church body? Also, it will be helpful if you know the *setting* for the negotiations. Ideally, you want to meet with no more than three or four individuals, in a setting conducive to a detailed discussion of the items at hand.

TARGETING YOUR PRIORITIES

Before sitting down to negotiate your Letter of Agreement, you must ask yourself some basic questions:
• What are my own personal priorities?

Is it to negotiate a significantly higher cash salary? To come to agreement on housing issues? To make sure you have adequate provisions for educational leave? You cannot negotiate with equal force on each and every provision in your Letter of Agreement. You must decide in advance which are the important items for you, and then devote your best efforts to reaching agreement on these key items.

• What is the minimum cash salary I will accept?

Richard Bolles, in his best-selling *What Color Is Your Parachute?* says that there are three key figures in any salary negotiation: (1) what you *need;* (2) what you *want;* and (3) what you will *settle for.*[3]

Before beginning salary negotiations, you need to be clear about what these three figures are for you, especially the third—the lowest minimum salary you will settle for, as a prerequisite for accepting a new position.

• Do I want a housing *allowance* or housing *supplied?*

There are advantages to each. If you and your family want to rent or purchase your own home, this is a decision that needs to be reached in advance of negotiations.

• Do I want a consultant to assist in negotiations?

In some denominations a consultant is required. If not, do you want such a person to be present?

WIN-WIN NEGOTIATING

"Win-Win" negotiating allows both parties to "win." The secret of win-win negotiating is to present *your* desires effectively, but to present them in such a way that the church sees an advantage to *them* in agreeing to your desires.

When negotiating for a higher starting salary, for example, the win-win negotiator might present the case in the following fashion:

"The position of senior pastor requires greater compensation than I see indicated in your preliminary figures. I know it is not easy to allocate additional money for this position. However, offering more money ultimately will work in your favor. A new pastor will tend to stay longer, will feel more positive about the church as well as about his or her ministry, and will be motivated to build a solid base of accomplishment that will benefit the church for years to come."

As you negotiate the various provisions of your Letter of Agreement, keep in mind the ways the church might benefit from adhering to your requests, and present your arguments accordingly.

We will now discuss the specific provisions contained in most clergy Letters of Agreement.

Position Description

The position description may be a part of your Letter of Agreement (in the "Duties" section), or it may be a separate document. It may contain a *general* list of duties, such as might apply to the senior pastor of any church, or, more rarely, it may specify certain goals to be accomplished by the new pastor. Finally, the position description need not necessarily be formulated in detail when you arrive, but may rather be worked out, by mutual agreement, at some specified time following your arrival. And it is simply smart planning to renegotiate your position description as often as once each year as you accomplish performance goals, or as you obtain new skills for ministry. Whatever procedure is used, a good position description possesses the following characteristics:

■ Mutuality

It states not only what *you* will do, but also how the congregation will support you in your ministry.

■ Specificity

It states *specific* goals and objectives to be achieved (not more than four to eight in number). It emphasizes results rather than activity. (Eating lunch with 10 parishioners last month is an activity, rather than a goal!)

■ Clarity

It states goals and objectives which are well-defined, clearly articulated, often measurable, and achievable.

■ Outer-oriented

It recognizes that the pastor's ministry is performing not only in the local church but also in the community and through the denomination.

SALARY AND BENEFITS

Specific items relating to salary and benefits should be addressed in your Letter of Agreement. These are discussed here *in the order in which they should be negotiated,* rather than the order in which they may appear on your agreement. For example, we start with clergy benefits before discussing housing and salary.

When negotiating individual items on your Letter of Agreement, keep in mind potential tax consequences.[4] For example, when paying pension, health, or life insurance premiums, if you are expected to share a proportion of the cost, it is to your advantage to have the church agree to assume the total cost, in exchange for a proportionate reduction of your salary, so that you will not pay income tax on items which represent a cost of doing ministry, rather than real income for you. (If too much resistance is apparent on such matters, the Internal Revenue Service does allow the use of health and dependent care reimbursement accounts. If you are filing taxes as a self-employed minister, you should be aware of the fact that the IRS is currently in the process of establishing numerous precedents that a church's payment of benefits should be added to the taxable income for self-employed clergy.)

In a similar fashion, continuing education and other professional expenses should be *separate line items* in the budget, not included in your salary, where they would be taxed to you as income.

As you review the following material, remember, as was said previously—*you cannot negotiate with equal weight each and every item on your Letter of Agreement. Decide in advance which are the priority items for you, and direct your efforts toward achieving a satisfactory resolution on these key items.*

Time of Work

Ideally, your agreement should specify a five-day work week, one of the working days to include Sunday. You should also be entitled to national holidays, as long as they do not conflict with the seasons of worship.

Vacation

A month's vacation, including Sundays, seems to be normative for clergy who serve in churches with white-collar or professional memberships, though most church members are able to secure only two or three weeks of paid vacation. Your negotiation should take into account the norms and practices of a particular congregation. You may want your agreement to define specifically what constitutes a month, as, for example, 23 working days, plus four (or five) Sundays.

Continuing Education

One to two weeks of leave time, plus $300 or more for educational expenses, seems to be normative. Your Letter of Agreement may also specify how much educational leave can be carried over from one year to another.

Sabbatical

Traditionally, the minister's sabbatical consisted of six months or more of leave after seven years in the church. A more flexible plan for providing a sabbatical would be for the church to agree to "set aside" a month's leave time for each year you are in the position, and also to place in an escrow account a month's expenses for supply clergy. Then, at an agreed upon time, some time between your third and seventh year, both time and money could be "drawn upon" to provide your sabbatical. If the church will not commit to providing a sabbatical, will they agree to discuss the possibility, at the end of your second full year at the church?

Other Leave Time

In additional to sick leave (discussed later), your agreement may also specify a certain amount of time off for family emergencies, illness or death in the family, or childbirth.

Social Security Reimbursement

Clergy are hurt financially, in that, while the IRS increasingly considers clergy to be employees of the church, they are considered self-employed when paying Social Security, and therefore pay the total amount themselves, rather than sharing the cost with an employer. To compensate, some churches agree to reimburse 50 percent or more of the pastor's Social Security taxes (SECA) directly to the pastor, as part of the pastor's taxable salary, and to designate this amount as a separate line item for Social Security reimbursement in the church budget. *Any* amount budgeted by the church for this purpose will have the advantage of putting church members on notice that clergy, unlike most church members, must pay the total amount of their Social Security taxes.

Pension and Pension Supplements

The church should agree to contribute to your denomination's pension plan on your behalf. To supplement your retirement income, you may want the church to agree to contribute to a Tax Deferred Annuity on your behalf, possibly available through your church pension fund.

Other Pension Benefits

Other benefits provided by some churches, depending upon the financial needs of the pastor, include provisions for a low-cost loan for down payment on a house or your children's college education, or a housing equity allowance (see "Clergy housing" later in this chapter).

Life And Health Insurance

Your congregation should agree to pay the premiums for family health insurance, group life, and dental insurance, if such coverage is mandated by your denomination.

Sickness, Disability, and Death

Your agreement should specify a reasonable amount of sick leave. In addition, you may want to encourage the church to subscribe to a Short Term Disability insurance policy, sometimes called income-replacement insurance. The advantage of this is that it provides benefits for you and your family in the event of short-term disability, so that the church can use the money set aside for your salary to pay a supply until you return. Your agreement should also state how long you and/or your family can remain in the parsonage during long-term disability, or in the event of your death.

Malpractice Insurance

While it is unlikely that the average pastor will ever be sued for malpractice, nevertheless, *if* you plan an extensive counseling ministry, you may want to consider malpractice coverage. In addition, if you plan to provide counseling for a fee, or in an employment situation separate from the church, you or your employer must acquire all necessary professional coverage. (While you are pondering, inquire into the viability of the congregation's liability coverage for the various programs, such as day care, prison ministry, or homeless ministry, which operate through the church.)

Auto and Travel

The church should agree to reimburse you for ministry-related auto and travel expenses. Preferable to the usual $200 or $300 monthly "auto allowance," is the provision of travel reimbursement, based on the IRS estimated cost per mile, or of a vehicle for your use, along with a gasoline credit card in the name of the church.

Office Expenses

The church should pay all costs involved in maintaining the church office. This includes the cost of your home-office phone.

Other Professional Expenses

Your agreement should provide reimbursement for your professional expenses, including the purchase of books, tapes, subscriptions to professional periodicals, dues for professional organizations, and attendance at church conventions, conferences, and meetings. You may even wish to have the church include a line item for home entertainment carried out as part of your professional duties, and also cover child-care expenses for situations when both you and your spouse are expected to attend church functions.

Discretionary Fund

Your agreement may provide for the establishment of a pastor's "discretionary fund" for use in pastoral emergencies, such as a parishioner's request for financial aid. Your agreement should state how the account is to be funded.

Supplementary Compensation

Many Letters of Agreement contain a statement that the minister is entitled to accept gifts for performing weddings, funerals, and baptisms. Naturally, the minister is also entitled to additional sources of income, whether received from writing, teaching, speaking, or consulting.

Moving Expenses

The church should agree to pay the full cost of your move, unless you and they have a prior agreement to share costs, or that there will be a "cap" on the church's share of the total costs. Moving expenses include also travel, meals, and lodging for any preliminary trips to the area, in advance of your actual move.

Use of Buildings

Your agreement should state who has final approval in granting permission for the use of church facilities by outside groups.

Starting Date

Your agreement needs to specify the official starting date on which your salary and benefits begin.

Revising Your Agreement

Your Letter of Agreement needs to specify the procedures to be followed to alter or amend it, noting that any such changes are to be made only by *mutual consent* at a *designated* time (such as at the time of the annual ministry review), and on an occasion *different* from that of your annual salary review.

Housing

Before discussing the housing provisions of your agreement, you and your family need to decide whether you prefer housing supplied by the church, or a housing allowance; second, you need to know whether the church is prepared to give you a choice in this matter.[5]

With Housing Supplied

Your agreement should state that the church will pay for upkeep and maintenance, utilities (including the phone), and major appliances. To insure that the house is adequately maintained, you may want your agreement to state that the church will conduct an annual inspection of the property, and that necessary repairs and maintenance will be completed following that inspection.

Even when the church provides housing, you are still entitled to have a portion of your salary designated as a housing allowance. This would cover the cost of furnishings and other items related to maintaining a home. Your agreement needs to specify the amount of this supplementary allowance.

Also, if you are to live in church-owned housing, you may wish to have the church designate an equity allowance, to compensate you for the equity you are losing by not owning your own home.

With a Housing Allowance

The fairest method for determining the amount of a housing allowance is for you and the church to agree on a total figure for salary and housing *combined*. You then determine, with the help of an individual knowledgeable about local real estate, the amount you are likely to spend on *all* housing-related expenses, including a down payment, mortgage payments, taxes, and maintenance. This amount is then designated by the church governing board as your housing allowance, the remainder being designated as salary.

The amount designated as housing allowance may change from year to year, depending upon your circumstances (for example, whether you are *purchasing* a house in any given year, and therefore need to budget in the amount for a down payment). Whatever amount is decided upon, it needs to be approved by the church board in advance for that calendar year.

If you do plan to buy your own home and lack the cash for a down payment, you may want your agreement to record how the church will help you in providing money for a down payment, perhaps in return for shared equity in the house. Under a *debenture* system, for example, church members contribute money for a down payment by purchasing "shares" of a loan, in return for shared equity in the house.

We have completed our discussion of the benefits to which you are entitled, and which need to be addressed in your Letter of Agreement. We turn now to the subject that, if the matter is still open, probably is of greatest concern to clergy who are negotiating a new call.

CASH SALARY

Before negotiating your cash salary with the church, you need to be clear in your own mind, as stated previously, about: (1) the probable *range* they are likely to offer; and (2) the *minimum figure* you are willing to accept within that range.

Arguments to Use

In presenting your case for adequate compensation, arguments could include the following:

■ Benefits to the Church

Clergy who are adequately compensated invest themselves fully in the life of the church, providing quality and continuity of leadership.

■ Qualifications

Your qualifications, including years of preparatory education, as well as X number of years in active ministry, should reward you with more compensation.

■ Denominational Guidelines

The church has a moral obligation to comply with published denominational salary guidelines, even if it is not required to do so.

■ Current Salary

Your new church is certainly not obligated to equal or exceed your current salary. However, from a common-sense point of view, the church certainly will understand that you are unlikely to consider a new position, if it pays less than what you are currently making.

Arguments Not to Use

■ Personal Need

Compensation for any position, in or out of the church, should be based on the demands of the position itself. It is simply not the church's concern whether you need extra income for that car payment or student loan.

■ Parity with Other Professionals

Clergy are not comparable to doctors, lawyers, or MBAs in terms of expected remuneration. Arguments to the effect that your compensation should equal that offered in other professional fields, even those present in the church, will simply make you look foolish, or worse—greedy.

SALARY REVIEW

In addition to specifying your starting salary, your Letter of Agreement should also state the process by which salary increases are determined. Terms to be addressed in connection with the salary review are the following:

■ When is the review *to be conducted?*

Your salary should be reviewed *annually*, and on a *different occasion* from your ministry review (see "ministry review," following).

■ Who *is involved?*

Does it include you as well as others?

■ What are the *criteria to be considered?*

Are salary increases to be based upon length of service, increases in the annual cost of living, measurable progress toward mutually agreed upon goals, or some combination of the above?

Finally, if the church is offering a starting salary below the minimum clergy compensation guidelines for your denomination, will the church commit itself, in writing, to achieving parity with denominational guidelines within a specified period of time, such as three years? When naming a figure to be achieved at the end of this period, remember to factor in the estimated cost of living increase during that period.

MINISTRY REVIEW

Provision for a periodic ministry review is the third major section of your Letter of Agreement.

Evaluation is a threatening word for many clergy, and often for good reason. Some clergy have been brutalized by ill-conceived and poorly conducted "evaluations." Therefore, it is important to have your agreement state certain basic understandings concerning the ministry review process:

■ It is a *mutual* process.

It is a review of the ministry of *clergy and laity together*, in the pursuit of previously identified goals and objectives.

■ It is an *aided* process.

It is to be conducted with the assistance of a *trained outside facilitator* or executive supervisor.

■ It is a process *separate from* the clergy salary review.

It is to be conducted at a different *time,* and with different *objectives* in mind.

It is not necessary that the ministry review be conducted annually. Some church professionals suggest that a comprehensive review be conducted every three to five years, following an initial review, which is conducted six months to a year after you start in a new position. Whatever timetable you and the church agree to follow, you should avail yourselves of some excellent resources for designing "non-toxic" and mutually beneficial ministry reviews.[6]

Termination

If the church's previous history suggests that involuntary termination may not be an unlikely possibility, you may want your agreement to contain some provisions to address this. Among them would be an agreement that the church will secure the services of a trained outside facilitator to mediate in situations of conflict, provisions for adequate severance pay, continuation of benefits for the pastor in the event of termination (suggested minimum: three months), and a guarantee of a minimum contract period (suggested: three years). Consult with a denominational official to draft the appropriate language for these provisions.

A NEW CHAPTER BEGINS

During the period when you are negotiating your Letter of Agreement, other issues and concerns are beginning to crowd in upon you. You are experiencing the emotional consequences of leaving your present ministry. You are looking forward, with excitement, but perhaps also with trepidation, to the challenges of your new position.

And you also are dealing with practical matters: announcing your resignation, saying good-bye, arranging for the move, and perhaps buying and selling houses. We will look at these and other matters in the next chapter, "Endings and Beginnings."

Chapter Nine

ENDINGS AND BEGINNINGS

"Let us go forth . . . for here we have no lasting city."

Hebrews 13:13a-14a (RSV)

Congratulations! You have been offered a new call and a new challenge. Understandably, you are eager to begin. At the same time, you and your family are being buffeted by conflicting emotions. You are about to embark on one of the most exciting, but at the same time, stress-filled periods of your life.

During the next year or so, you will terminate your relationship with your present church, initiate a new ministry, and move from one city, or even from one region of the country, to another. Or you may be moving a few miles down the road in just three months. If, from time to time, you and your family feel overwhelmed, it is understandable.

In this chapter, we will look at the challenges—professional and personal—that will face you and your family during this critical period of transition.[1]

Immediately after the search committee or denominational executive has informed you that you have received a new call, and when you have accepted that call, the first stress-filled event you may experience is a case of . . .

"Buyer's Remorse"

A term from real estate, "buyer's remorse" refers to feelings of doubt and uncertainty that result from making a major life decision, such as buying a new house or, in the case of clergy, accepting a new call. Clergy suffering from buyer's remorse have even been known to phone their prospective church and cancel their call.

To deal with buyer's remorse, realize that it is, to one degree or another, a normal reaction to any major life decision. If you find yourself experiencing severe doubts about your decision to accept a new call, get back in touch with the reasons you sought out this new opportunity in the first place. The more objectively you can identify why you wanted to move, and what attracted you to this new position, the less likely you will be to fall a victim of buyer's remorse.

117

Once you have definitely accepted a new call, your next step is, of course . . .

Tendering Your Resignation

Do not resign, or even hint at the possibility of leaving, until your new call is official. When your Letter of Agreement has been finalized, or after denominational officials have rubber-stamped the placement process, announce your leaving to your present congregation, allowing approximately six to eight weeks from the time of your announcement until your planned departure. Announce your resignation in the following manner, allowing approximately one week from start to finish:

• Privately inform the head of your church board.
• Announce your resignation to the board at large.
• Following the board meeting, tell friends and the heads of major parish organizations.
• Announce to the whole congregation the next Sunday, followed up by a letter to all church members.

Terminating with Your Present Church

The six to eight weeks until your departure is one of the most important times of your ministry. The quality and style of your leave-taking will determine, in large part, whether you and your former church face the future unencumbered by emotional baggage of the past. Roy Oswald, in his excellent book *Running Through the Thistles,* makes the point that clergy often rely on their "instincts" when choosing the style and manner of their leave-taking, but that our instincts seldom point the way to an effective termination.[2] One counterproductive style Oswald describes as "running through the thistles." Clergy may deny the emotional pain of leave-taking by attempting to "run through it" as quickly as possible. Another style is the "sponge approach." Clergy may listen empathetically and "soak up" expressions of pain on the part of church members, but never share their own feelings about their departure.

Characteristics of an Effective Termination

In contrast to these two counterproductive termination styles, an effective termination has the following characteristics:

Intentionality

Do not rely on instinct, but rather on a carefully thought-out plan.

Decisiveness

Put church members on notice that you will not be coming back for weddings, funerals, or other pastoral duties, except at the expressed invitation of the new pastor.

Kindness

Present your reasons for leaving in the best possible light. Even a "lateral move" can be explained on the basis of providing greater opportunities to perform a particular style of ministry that is suited to your own gifts as you perceive them.

Taking Care of Details

Leave the church in good shape for the next pastor. Bring membership records up to date, fill committee chairmanships and Christian education teaching posts, and compose an orientation letter for your successor.

Celebrating the Past and Looking Toward the Future

Allow members to celebrate your time together, perhaps by means of an all-church dinner or going-away party. Worship can also help make the transition. *Ritual in a New Day: An Invitation* contains a specific liturgy for the leave-taking of a pastor.[3] Finally, your preaching during the last few Sundays can highlight the unity of the church in Christ, rather than in any one minister.

Dealing with Stress

While you are terminating with your present church and simultaneously planning your move, you and your family will probably be experiencing considerable emotional stress. Remember, stress is the result of *any major change* in your life, even positive changes. It is important, therefore, that you and your family follow some stress-management procedures during your transition:

• Talk about what you are feeling.

Share your sense of excitement—and also your fears—about this transition.

• Use time and energy wisely.

Plan your move. Don't allow uncompleted tasks to bunch up at the end.

• Maintain familiar routines.

There is comfort in familiar routines, especially when everything else in your life seems to be changing.

• Watch your health.

Eat right, sleep right, and try not to become stressed and overtired.

• Go on vacation.

If you can arrange it, take some vacation time before you begin your new position. This will be a time of relaxation, but also for reflecting on the past and preparing for the future.

Family Stress

Your family may actually be under more stress than you, both during and after the move. For one thing, they themselves have not initiated the move, and therefore may feel anger and resentment at being uprooted. Second, clergy moves often take place during the summer, tearing children away from their friends and isolating them in a strange town, months before school begins. Finally, clergy step into a ready-made routine in their new church, whereas family members are left on their own to make new friends and to establish new routines.

Help your family deal with the stress of the move by taking time to listen to them. Let them talk about their feelings. Spend "quality time" with them during this period. Maintain familiar routines. A good picture book may help inform younger children about what the move involves.[4] Older children may need to hear that you are willing to make arrangements to visit former friends. In general, allow time to give your family strong emotional support during the days and weeks before and after the move.

Preparing for Your New Church

If the church that has called you is significantly different from your present church—that is, if it is substantially larger or of a different character from your present ministry—these last few weeks are a good time to seek out a pastor who is currently serving a similar church in your area, to explore the issues that will be facing you. Be sure that the person you seek out is one who has successfully resolved these issues, not one who has been defeated by them.

Buying and Selling a House

If you are selling a house, obtain a competitive market analysis from at least three reputable brokers. Subsequently, select one of the three to represent you. For a quick sale, consider a 30- or 60-day listing. If you are considering renting your house out for a period of time before you sell it, be aware that you must sell it within two years in order to avoid capital-gains taxes.

The long-term trend is for clergy to own their own homes. If you plan to buy when you move to your new church, you will be able to qualify for a mortgage that is up to two and one half times your total family income. This would include the total of your cash salary, your housing allowance, your Social Security offset, if offered, and your spouse's salary. It would not include supplementary benefits such as pension premiums. In other words, if the total of the above figures is $40,000, you will be able to qualify for a mortgage of up to $100,000. Even though the church may designate a certain proportion of your total salary as a housing allowance, the formula used to qualify for a mortgage will be based upon a percentage of your total income, less debts—not upon the figure designated by the church for housing.

If, like many clergy, you have little or no money for a down payment, you could explore the possibility of a gift or loan from a relative, a VA or an FHA loan, which require a smaller down payment, or an equity-sharing arrangement with your church (see the "housing" section of chapter 8). Talk to your real estate agent for details about these and other financing options.

Moving

Benjamin Franklin is reported to have said, "Three moves equal one fire." In order to make *your* move less traumatic, you and your spouse need to decide in advance who is going to do what. Among the major tasks that need to be completed are the following:[5]

■ Send out change-of-address cards to:
____ magazines
____ newspapers
____ friends
____ firms where you have charge accounts
____ local post office branch
____ draft board

■ Transfer records:
____ church
____ school
____ bank or savings and loan
____ insurance companies
____ doctors and dentists (prescription refills?)
____ organizations
____ lawyer
____ automobile and driver's license

■ Notify home-delivery services:

To stop service at old address:		To start service at new address:
____	telephone company	____
____	electric power company	____
____	water company	____
____	gas company	____
____	milk delivery	____
____	newspapers/magazines	____
____	laundry	____
____	trash collector	____
____	water-softener service	____

____ have rugs and carpets cleaned and chemically treated if they are going into storage
____ return borrowed tools, books, etc.
____ make firm decisions on what you are taking and leaving

____ advertise or arrange to sell some items
____ call charitable organizations to give away furniture, clothing, toys, etc.

Some movers advertise special discounts for members of the clergy. These discounts, however, may be no different from the discounts routinely offered to other customers.

In order to cut costs on your move, consider packing your books yourself and shipping them by parcel post. This is actually cheaper than having them moved professionally. Also remember to take your old phone books with you.

For more detailed information on preparing for a move, I recommend Carolyn Janik's *Positive Moves: The Complete Guide to Moving You and Your Family Across Town or Across the Nation.*[6]

YOU HAVE ARRIVED AT THE NEW CHURCH

The First Few Days

You have finally arrived! The boxes have been unpacked (at least some of them) and you are ready to begin this new chapter in your life. One of the most useful things you can do during your first few days in your new church is take a few minutes and walk around your physical plant. Notice anything that seems strange or out of place. If you do not take note of these things when you first arrive, you will soon get used to them, as your church members already have.

Feelings of stress and overload are common during the early stage of a new ministry. As much as possible, keep to an ordinary routine and have recourse to stress reduction activities that have worked for you in the past. If a quiet walk in the woods or a few hours in the local library have proved rejuvenating in the past, find time for this during your first few days in the new location.

"Getting to Know You"

"Getting to know you"—so go the words of a popular song. During the first few days and weeks in a new call, you will get to know the members of the congregation, and they will get to know you. This is a time of lasting "first impressions" on both sides.

One of the most helpful things said to me when I started in a new church several years ago was this: "The reputation you establish during your first six months here is probably the reputation you will live with for a long time."

In the early days of your new ministry, people will be taking notice of your personal style. Do you meet people in an open and engaging manner? Do you express little social amenities that say to people, "I like you. I *care* about you"? Do you look people in the eye and give them a firm handshake? Do you care about their children? Do you seem organized and in control of your work? Do you return calls and respond to pastoral requests? Do you show up on time for meetings? Do you keep regular office hours? Do you visit people in the hospital? Again, the reputation you establish during your first six months will stay with you for a long time.

Your first few weeks in the church give you an opportunity to let the congregation know more about you and your family. Put a brief biographical sketch in the church newsletter. Tell the congregation what you want them to know about your work schedule, such as that your day off is Monday and, barring emergencies, that you prefer to be contacted at the church office rather than at home.

Your first few weeks are also a marvelous opportunity to visit your new members. You will never have this much time for visiting again. Furthermore, calling on key members during this period will make a big impression, both on those visited and on the general church membership when they hear about your visits.

During the first few weeks, you also should make a point of attending meetings of church groups and organizations. Explain that you probably will not be able to meet with them on a regular basis in the future but, this first time, you wanted to meet with them and learn about their activities. Make an effort to get to know the paid staff at the church during this period. Taking them out to lunch is a good first step.

If the former pastor is still living in the community, and perhaps even intends to remain a member of the congregation, meet with this person shortly after you arrive. Discuss what will happen if a longtime member requests this former pastor to officiate at a wedding or funeral. It needs to be understood that major pastoral functions are now to be performed by you, although the former pastor can certainly assist, with your permission.

Listen . . . Listen . . . Listen . . .

One of the most important tasks during the early stage of your ministry is listening. As you call on church members and get acquainted with the congregation as a whole, you will be asking, in your own mind, such questions as: How does the congregation feel about itself? What is its "self-image"? How does it see its mission and role? Which individuals and groups really possess the "power" in the church, and should be consulted before you consider any major changes? Listening carefully to congregational needs, as they are revealed by parishioners during the first few months of your new ministry, will help to guard against the tendency to launch immediately into tried and true programs that have worked for you in the past.

During the early stages of your new ministry, you may also find yourself listening to endless stories about the previous pastor. Listen patiently. These stories are not implied criticisms of you. They are simply ways in which members of the congregation are working through their feelings of grief about the previous pastor's departure.

What the "Honeymoon" *Really* Is

Every pastor has heard of the so-called "honeymoon period" that occurs during the first few months in a new church. This is supposedly the time when new pastors can do no wrong in the eyes of the congregation.

Research published by The Alban Institute has cast some interesting new light on this "honeymoon period."[7] Rather than being a period of unconditional favorable regard of the new pastor, the "honeymoon period" is really a time of noncommunication, during which the new pastor is not yet trusted enough to be given honest feedback. This is not a time, therefore, for initiating major changes—in worship or in any other aspects of the life of the congregation. It is rather a time for building trust between you and the congregation, and establishing a firm foundation for future ministry.

Instituting Change

If, as I suggested, the "honeymoon period" is not a time for instituting major changes in the life of the congregation, then when is?

In general, change should occur after you have earned the trust of the congregation. Changes in worship are especially sensitive. Maintaining the familiar worship style is a matter of enormous importance to a majority of members of the congregation. The general consensus of pastors is that changes in worship should not be attempted for the first six months to two years of a new pastorate.[8] Unless changes are appropriately timed and carefully prepared for, they have the potential for arousing enormous anger and resentment.

When you have earned the trust of the congregation, and you believe it is time to take your first major initiative, choose the focus of that initiative very carefully. The congregation will give a great deal of attention to the area you choose to emphasize, and will tend to give your initiative in this area a broader-based support than possible subsequent initiatives. Therefore, choose an area of importance for the future health and vitality of the congregation, rather than some favorite pet project of your own.

Women's Start-up Issues

Female clergy who start in a new parish face most of the same start-up issues a man faces, in addition to some that arise as a result of their gender.

One of these gender issues is confused role expectation on the part of church members. You may be asked to do certain things, or to perform your job in a certain way, that would not be expected of a man. It may be suggested that you personally type the bulletin, for example, or that you surrender conducting the meetings of the church board to someone who is "more experienced," and who probably also happens to be male. Your general rule is not to perform your professional duties differently from the way a man would be expected to perform them in similar circumstances.

Another major issue for female clergy starting a new position is professional isolation. For this reason, it is extremely important for women to build a support group during their first few weeks and months in a new parish. In addition, if you can find a mentor, someone who can give you professional guidance and personal support, this will be very useful. Although a natural tendency for many female clergy will be to choose a female mentor, a male pastor may be able to provide more objective feedback concerning whether an issue you are facing is gender-specific, or one commonly experienced by most pastors in a new congregation.

YOUR INSTITUTION

Your formal institution as the new pastor of the church marks a new chapter in your life. It also marks a new chapter in the life of the congregation.

When planning the service, personalize it as much as possible. State the style and emphasis of your intended ministry by your choice of the preacher, the "gifts" to be presented, the Scripture readings, the music, and, of course, the liturgy. Remember also that your ministry extends beyond the immediate congregation, so invite community leaders and local clergy from other denominations to participate. If possible, arrange in advance to have someone other than yourself serve as chief liturgical officer or "master of ceremonies," so that you are not orchestrating the troops at your own party.

Consider having the members of the search committee or parish relations committee assist with planning your institution or installation. Their involvement not only would help you organize the service, it also would be a way of ratifying their call to you as pastor.

A spirited and well-conducted institution affirms the past, celebrates the present, and sets the stage for a fruitful new ministry.

ON TO THE FUTURE!

As the first weeks and months of your new ministry pass, you will discover that you are no longer the "new kid on the block." You and the congregation will begin to grow in a sense of mutual trust. Eventually, the time of transition will be over, and you will begin the process of creating a new ministry.

In preparation for this new ministry, invite the congregation to participate with you in writing a mission goal statement for the church. A good time for this is approximately a year after you arrive. A well-crafted mission goal statement captures a sense of the distinctive quality of a congregation's mission, while it articulates a focus for your common ministry in the years ahead.

Chapter Ten

CREATIVE SOLUTIONS FOR WOMEN, MINORITIES, AND 55-AND-OVER CLERGY

We are what he has made us, created in Christ Jesus for good works.

Ephesians 2:10

Certain clergy experience greater than usual problems in placement. Among these are:

- female clergy
- racial and ethnic minority clergy
- clergy 55 and over
- singles and/or divorced clergy
- clergy couples
- terminated clergy
- short-tenured clergy
- reentry clergy
- "downsizing" clergy (i.e., wanting to move to a smaller church)

In this chapter, I will discuss practical strategies for *all* clergy in the hard-to-place categories. Then in the second portion of the chapter, I will discuss particular guidelines for each category.

PLACEMENT STRATEGIES

Don't be apologetic.

Before you face your first search committee, get back in touch with who you are and why you were called to ministry. Remind yourself of your gifts for ministry, and the ways you have used them effectively. In fact, you must first be convinced that you are a viable candidate before you set out to convince others.

Do all the right things.

Be clear about the ministry you are seeking, present yourself effectively on paper and in person, pursue all potential leads, and be aggressive in your search until you secure a new position.

Be highly pro-active.

Don't wait for opportunities to come knocking. Actively seek them out. Keep in close contact with your denominational placement officer. Maintain contact with prospective churches. Above all, set aside a *regular time each week* for placement-related tasks.

Take advantage of all placement channels.

Every denomination has both formal and informal placement channels, as was mentioned in chapter 5. The formal channels operate through prescribed procedures. The informal channels operate largely through word of mouth. The successful candidate will take full advantage of both formal and informal channels.

Maintain high visibility.

Search out opportunities to serve on denominational committees. If you are not currently serving a church, make yourself available for Sunday supply or interim work. Work continuously to make yourself a publicly visible member of your denomination.

Build a support network.

No matter what your situation, remind yourself that you are not alone. There are other people in your circumstances, dealing with the same frustrations and challenges. Find out who some of these people are and what has worked for them. You may learn that there are conferences on the national level, or support groups on the local level, for female clergy, for clergy couples, or for other clergy in circumstances similar to your own.

Be creative and flexible.

Flexibility and a willingness to consider a variety of options will work to your advantage. Be willing to relocate. Enlarge the geographic scope of your search. Enlarge your perceptions of the type of church you are willing to serve. Consider part-time, bivocational, or interim ministry.

Consider appointive positions.

It is often easier to be hired by one individual than by a committee. Appointive positions on the staff of a large church or denomination headquarters also have the potential of leading to subsequent elective positions for which you might previously not have been considered qualified.

Convert liabilities to assets.

If you are over 55, for example, tell search committees that you possess a wealth of experience in ministry, as well as the special ability to relate to the older members of the congregation. If you are divorced, point out that your situation has given you greater sensitivity to all who have suffered disruptions in their personal lives. Whatever your "liability," convert it into a potential plus to further your candidacy.

Don't force the issue.

Ultimately, you want to be called by or appointed to a church that can accept you fully and completely as their pastor.

Therefore, if you discover that a particular search committee has real difficulty with your candidacy, do not bend over backward to "convince" them. Simply accept that this is not the church for you, and move on.

FEMALE CLERGY

In spite of several decades of being ordained in the mainstream denominations, women continue to encounter a glass ceiling when they attempt to move from their first position as staff associate to senior pastor of a congregation. What can women do to maximize their opportunities?

Be positive and upbeat.

The reality, in today's clergy job market, is that women may expect to be interviewed for a disproportionate number of small congregations. Therefore, during the interview with such congregations, the effective female candidate will use statements such as, "There is a lot that can be done here. I see great potential. There is so much we can do together."

Come across as firm and in control.

Present yourself and your ideas in a direct and forthright manner. Avoid the use of qualifying words and phrases such as "hopefully" and "Don't you think that . . . ?" Enter and close with a firm handshake. Maintain good eye contact throughout.

Be aware of larger power issues.

Some lay leaders may favor a female candidate out of the belief that they can "control" her more easily than a male minister. Use the interview to communicate, politely and firmly, that you would be in charge of your ministry. You would chair the board of deacons meetings, if this is the custom in your denomination, and you do not plan to type the Sunday bulletin.

Be responsive to unspoken concerns.

Female candidates are often resentful (rightfully so) of questions relating to personal and family life, questions that might be interpreted differently if a male were answering. The problem is that such issues, whether raised in the interview or not, are of concern to search committee members, and if they are not addressed, you may be passed over in favor of another candidate—often male—about whom no lingering doubts remain.

Therefore, it may be to the advantage of female candidates to *deliberately bring up unspoken concerns* such as, "Who would take care of the children when they are sick?" or "What would happen if your spouse were relocated?" and resolve them to the satisfaction of the search committee.

Another issue you need to get on the table is, "What would be the reaction of church members if a woman were called?" This issue also needs to be resolved in the minds of search committee members before they will be able to accept you as a viable candidate.

Help them see your gender as a plus.

Among the arguments you can present are the following: A woman often is more collegial in leadership style. A woman pastor can relate to certain groups in the church more easily than a man—teenage girls needing a role model, women in troubled marriages. A woman tends to be aware of different *issues* in the church and the community, and therefore may be able to lead the church into whole new areas of ministry.

Consider interim ministry.

The challenge for women in the ministry is to be perceived as potential leaders of a congregation. For this reason, many women have found interim ministry an effective way to build a solid track record of successful congregational leadership, in preparation for seeking subsequent positions.

Do not settle for less than you are worth.

Women have the advantage that, depending upon family and other circumstances, they can sometimes consider a position that a male candidate could not. However, you do not want to "come cheap." Talk to your placement officer to find out what would be considered fair compensation for the position. Then negotiate a settlement package that reflects this. Some female clergy, during childbearing years, tend to agree to a part-time arrangement on the staff of a church. The tendency on this kind of "Mommy track" is to negotiate for part-time hours and pay, but then gradually become consumed by full-time work, especially when the senior pastor is away for a month. A part-time job in professional ministry is very difficult to describe or limit.

MINORITY CLERGY

The problem for African American and other minority clergy is getting themselves considered for a full range of positions in the church. Here are some suggestions:

Expand your expectations.

Many black and minority candidates assume that they will never serve a mixed-race, or even a primarily white congregation. Don't make this assumption. Expand your expectations to include any church that has the characteristics you are looking for, without regard for the racial background of the congregation.

Bag your anger.

Minority candidates naturally feel angry when confronted with institutional racism, especially in clergy placement. However, unresolved anger against "the system" will tend to work against presenting yourself effectively to potential churches, where you can work from the inside to continue the needed change.

Become visible in your denomination.

Serve on denominational committees. Chair those committees, if possible. Become known and visible throughout your nomination, not just in your local community.

Lobby your placement officer.

Encourage your denominational executives to recommend black and minority candidates, including yourself, for a full range of positions in the church.

Make full use of mainstream placement channels.

The black and other minority clergy "networks" work only for black and minority positions. If you want to be considered for a full range of opportunities, make full use of the mainstream placement channels in your denomination.

Learn from those who have gone where you want to go.

Seek out individuals in your denomination who have achieved the kind of positions you would like to achieve. Find out what worked for them, and how you might apply it to your situation.

Consider appointive positions.

As stated previously, it is often easier to be hired by one person than by a committee. Many appointive positions have excellent salaries and high levels of responsibility. When being considered for staff positions, your racial diversity will often work in your favor.

Learn the "language" of the other culture.

When interviewing it is important to speak the "language" of the other culture. White middle-class congregations often prefer a more enabling, collegial style of leadership than the strong pastor-centered model typical of many African American congregations.

Be aware of such cultural differences when presenting yourself in an interview.

Develop a high tolerance for frustration.

Being considered for a wider range of opportunities in the church is an uphill battle. Many times, you will be interviewed as the "token minority." Again and again, you will conduct what you believe to be an effective interview and will be passed over. The final prize goes to those who persevere in spite of frustration.

Encourage other minority members to enter the ministry.

Real progress in minority clergy placement will only come when there is a "critical mass" of such clergy in the church. Encouraging other minority members to enter the ministry is an investment in progress for the next generation.

All things considered in this age of diversity and cultural fragmentation, and if God is leading you, it is not reprehensible to eventually consider switching to a different denominational environment, where you will be more welcome. On the one hand, avoid the tendency to think that the grass is greener elsewhere. Sometimes it is. On the other hand, don't confuse loyalty with a false sense of security.

CLERGY 55 AND OVER

In spite of what you may have heard, the job market is by no means closed to clergy in their mid-50s or over. In some mainstream denominations, the average age of clergy is over 50!

The first task is to overcome age barriers in your mind. Ask yourself, How do I feel about my age? If necessary, do a mock interview with a colleague. Afterward, get their reactions about how you handled questions relating to your age, and how you might handle these more effectively.

Second, as has been said previously, present your "disadvantages" as advantages. As a seasoned pastor, you offer the church a vital combination of experience and ability that would be an asset to any congregation.

SINGLES AND/OR DIVORCED CLERGY

Single clergy have always experienced discrimination that counters placement in the church. An unspoken fear of single clergy probably has increased in recent years, especially for single male clergy, as a result of the fear of AIDS.

Single clergy should self-confidently present themselves on the strength of their proven gifts for ministry. If you present yourself sufficiently well, this will overcome any regrets that "we will not have a family in the parsonage."

For divorced clergy, a single divorce is no longer the impediment to placement that it once was. Multiple divorces, however, continue to present problems in most denominations. In either case, if at all possible, do not seek a new call while undergoing a divorce. Instead, stay in your present church and put your job search on hold until you regain stability in your personal life.

In some denominations or churches, and depending upon the circumstances, cultural mores will not allow you to stay in your present position indefinitely during a divorce. If possible, try to negotiate either for a severance package or for several months in which to get your life reordered.

CLERGY COUPLES

Clergy couples typically employ one of four strategies when making plans for a new call. One, you can proceed on a first-come, first-served basis. Two, you can proceed on a your-turn, my-turn basis. Three, you can proceed on a seniority basis, where the one with the senior position takes first priority in placement. Four, you can seek a joint call or appointment, which means a form of job sharing. Proceeding on a seniority basis usually will make the most sense financially, but it usually also will tend to favor the male candidate as the one with the senior position.

If you are committed to seeking a *shared* position as coministers, plan to spend more time on the search and also to extend your search over a wider geographic area. Even so, there is no guarantee that you will succeed in obtaining a position as copastors of the same church. Appointment of copastors in closed systems is a preferred choice, but there may not be enough midsized churches to meet the demand.

If you *are* seeking a position as copastors, use your written materials and, later, the interview, to present to the church the potential benefits of shared ministry. Among these would be a more diverse gift mix, a greater opportunity for *all* members of the congregation to relate to the clergy leadership team, and flexibility of time and schedule (If one of you is out of town, the other is available).

During the interview, be prepared to explain how you would share responsibilities, and which one of you would be the "boss."

If you *are* called as copastors, make sure that your Letter of Agreement clearly spells out total hours to be worked and areas of accountability, so that the two of you do not end up being "two for the price of one."

Clergy couples in some denominations have formed networks and willingly share experiences, if not strategies.

TERMINATED, SCANDAL-RIDDEN, OR PROBLEM-PLAGUED CLERGY

One bad placement can happen to anyone. If you have been terminated by a church, make every attempt not to carry your anger into an interview with another church. Present the facts of your termination as favorably as you can. Say, for example, that your previous ministry was productive in many ways, but that ideological differences between you and the congregation finally necessitated a mutual decision to separate. Second, enlist the aid of a denominational official to serve as your advocate. This person can present your side of the case without the appearance of self-interest.

If, however, you have been involved in a scandal in the church and are attempting to return to full-time ministry, plan to do so over a period of time. Begin by accepting supply preaching assignments. When the time seems appropriate, present yourself to denominational officials to be considered for a new position. In reality, the potential for litigation will make it increasingly difficult for individuals with a history of sexual impropriety to be considered for future positions in the church.

Finally, if your termination or forced resignation was simply the last in a series of such events, explore with a denominational official or a qualified pastoral counselor whether God may be calling you to other work. Your denomination may pay for a career assessment at one of the church-related career development centers listed in appendix D of this book. Then turn to the next chapter to explore alternative career options.

SHORT-TENURED CLERGY

Clergy who have moved frequently may trigger concern in a search committee. When preparing your placement materials, consider listing several short-term positions within a time frame of five to seven years. This way, your record of employment will appear more stable. During the interview, be willing to give reasonable assurances that, if called, you will commit to staying for an appropriate length of time.

REENTRY CLERGY

If you are reentering the active ministry after a period of secular employment, emphasize your church involvements, even though they may have been part-time. List, but deemphasize your secular employment. Consider a combination functional and chronological résumé, as described in chapter 4. Such a résumé would enable you to present your secular experience in terms of the leadership qualities needed for congregational ministry. During the interview, emphasize that the experience and gifts you demonstrated in the secular world are strong assets for future ministry.

"DOWNSIZING" CLERGY

Clergy who are seeking a *smaller*, rather than a large, church may trigger fears in a search committee that their desire is a symptom of personal or professional problems, such as marital conflict, substance abuse, or simple laziness.

Your best strategy is to move the focus of the discussion off the *size* of the church, and onto its *characteristics*. State, for example, that your number-one desire for this next stage of your ministry is to serve a church where you can be personally involved in the lives of all the members of your congregation. You will probably get credit for being the only pastor the church has interviewed who is not excessively "career-minded"!

Special Gifts

In this chapter we have discussed placement strategies for hard-to-place candidates in the church. We have emphasized the importance of persistence, flexibility, and a willingness to consider a variety of options. As a placement officer, I firmly believe that, whatever your circumstances—whether you are a woman, a member of a racial or ethnic minority, over 55, or have been terminated—you *can* succeed in obtaining a position in the church and, in so doing, can change your "impediment" into a unique and special gift for ministry.

Chapter Eleven

CAREER ALTERNATIVES FOR THOSE WHO WANT OUT

Now there are varieties of gifts . . . and there are varieties of working.

I Corinthians 12:4*a*, 6*a* (RSV)

It would be a rare clergyperson who had never given serious thought to the possibility of leaving the profession for secular work. Reliable statistics are hard to come by, but it is probable that as many as one-fifth of all clergy have thought seriously about the possibility of leaving the ministry, at some point in their career. Women consider this option more often after their first church, when they encounter less mobility in a vocation dominated by men. In addition, a growing number of clergy have lost their positions as a result of termination, forced resignation, or budget cuts.

If you are contemplating an exit from the ministry for secular work, first ask yourself one fundamental question:

• What is the problem for which leaving the ministry is the solution?

Problems often mentioned by clergy include the following:

■ poor compensation
■ lack of satisfaction in the work
■ burn-out
■ feeling that one's gifts could be better used elsewhere
■ a strong attraction to an alternative line of work.

Ask yourself, in all honesty, which of these problems, or another one not listed, is the real reason for *you*? Once you have answered this question to your satisfaction, ask yourself a second question:

• Other than leaving the ministry, what would be a solution to your problem?

Suppose, for example, that you are basically happy in parish ministry, but you and your family simply cannot live on the salary the church provides. Solutions other than leaving the ministry would include seeking a call to a larger church, generating additional income through part-time employment, or encouraging your spouse to seek employment.

140

If your problem, instead, is that parish ministry does not provide sufficient scope for your personal interest, such as teaching or counseling, could you seek such opportunities in the community, or through your denomination?

If, however, potential solutions to your particular problem leave you cold, and you still find yourself contemplating leaving the ordained ministry, then perhaps a career change is indicated. In addition, there are clergy who, through circumstances beyond their control, are *forced* to seek new work, either in or out of the church.

IF YOU HAVE BEEN FIRED

If you have been fired or have resigned under pressure, you face the same issues as any person who has lost a job. You must (a) come to terms with the financial and emotional consequences of unemployment; (b) negotiate the best possible termination settlement; (c) establish an interim source of income; and (d) decide whether you want to continue in your present field—ministry—or begin the transition into another type of work.

If you *have* been fired, work closely with a denominational representative (or if you are an independent pastor, seek an outside consultant/arbitrator) to negotiate the best possible termination settlement with your former church, and also to make plans for your future. Then go to your local library and obtain a copy of *CONGRATULATIONS! You've Been Fired* by Emily Koltnow and Lynne S. Dumas, to explore the emotional and practical consequences of your termination.[1]

Whether your leaving the ordained ministry was intentional or not, however, your next step is to . . .

COUNT THE COST

Leaving the ministry is not without cost. You need to be clear about what these costs are, and how you will deal with them. The costs include:

Loss of Income
Clergy often receive generous benefits that more than double the value of their cash compensation. If you are currently earning $25,000,

you would need to earn as much as $50,000 or more in salary and benefits, in order to equal what you are currently making.

Loss of Identity

Clergy have a professional identity that is powerfully connected with their personal identity. Reportedly, clergy are similar to military personnel in the strength of their professional identity, and in the difficulty they experience in leaving this identity behind.

Loss of Credibility

Clergy often discover that their motives are questioned when they attempt to leave the church. Also, the popular image of clergy as impractical and unworldly creates difficulties in being taken seriously as candidates for positions in the secular world.

Loss of Seniority

Clergy entering another type of work usually have to start at the bottom of the ladder. The two exceptions are clergy who have prior experience in another field, and those who leave the church to become executive directors of nonprofit agencies.

ALTERNATIVE CAREERS

What do clergy do when they are no longer employed in the church? One often hears sad stories about unemployed ministers driving taxis or bagging groceries. In reality, individuals who have been employed in a responsible, professional capacity such as the ministry, and who probably have college, and even graduate training, should not need to accept a position below the professional level unless they choose to do so. The problem with clergy who find themselves underemployed after leaving parish ministry is usually not lack of *qualifications*. It is lack of *imagination*. They do not perceive what they could do, other than the ordained ministry, and do not believe themselves qualified for anything else. Clergy considering secular work need to clearly identify what they wish to do, and they need to believe themselves qualified for it.

What alternative occupations *are* clergy well qualified for? Dr. Roy Lewis, executive director of the Northeast Career Center in Princeton, New Jersey, believes that clergy are well suited for jobs that involve helping, teaching, or leading others, which would include the following:[2]

- Teaching: college, public schools, private schools
- Personnel
- Counselor: outplacement, rehabilitation service, marriage and family, psychology and psychotherapy
- Service Industries: conference manager for hotels, public relations, advertising, demonstrator
- Fund Raising: part of funding firm, development personnel for nonprofits (i.e., college, university, hospital, nursing homes)
- Sales: insurance, product representative, financial planner
- Federal, State, Local Government Positions: trainer, investigator, manpower specialist, arbitrator
- CEO: nonprofit sector
- Librarian
- Writer: editing, publishing, journalism

Transition from one occupation to another, such as from the ministry to teaching, is possible because we possess what career counselors call *transferable skills.* These are skills that can be, literally, "transferred" from one occupation to another. Clergy who want to move into secular work need to realize that they possess transferable skills and that these skills can be used in occupations other than the ministry. The most important question for clergy considering transitioning is, What do you *want* to do? Identifying an alternative occupation is a three-step process, which involves reflecting, exploring, and investigating.

Reflecting

Reflect seriously on what God is calling you to do with your life. One way to do this is by means of written exercises designed to get you in touch with your deepest values, interests, and abilities. One favorite is "A Perfect Day," described in chapter 3. Other similar exercises are described in the same chapter, and also in *What I REALLY Want To Do: How to Discover the Right Job.*[3]

Once you have identified some alternative occupations that interest you, your next step is . . .

Exploring

Find out more about these occupations. A valuable resource is the *Occupational Outlook Handbook,* a compendium of jobs in the American economy, published by the Bureau of Labor Statistics in Washington, D.C., and revised every two years. Available in the "Reference" section of your library, the *O.O.H.* provides a description of the work you may be considering, as well as information about where such jobs are found, the training required, salary levels, and employment outlook.

After you have consulted the *O.O.H.* about alternative occupations, your next step is . . .

Investigating

Get a personal feel for what it is like to perform this work. The best way to do this is to conduct an *informational interview.*.

Suppose, for example, that you are considering the work of a full-time pastoral counselor. You identify a person who is currently performing this work and set up a time to meet together. You then ask this person certain basic questions: What do they especially enjoy about the work? What do they *not* enjoy? What training is necessary? Where are jobs to be found? What are employment prospects? What are the financial realities of working in this field? (Some pastors wish that they had taken this approach to a life of ordained ministry before they began theological education!)

After your informational interview, ask yourself some common sense questions: How do you feel about the work after talking to this person? Were you at all "turned on"? Would you enjoy doing the things your interview subject seems to enjoy? Is there a match between your gifts and abilities and those required in this field?

Continue with your informational interviewing of different prospects until you have identified what God is calling you to do, as an alternative to congregational ministry.

GETTING HIRED

A visit to your local bookstore will reveal no shortage of books available on all aspects of job hunting, from writing a résumé to conducting an interview. Rather than covering the same ground, I will focus my remarks on issues of importance to clergy who seek a transition into secular work.

Résumé

Your church résumé will not work for going into secular work. Rewrite a combination chronological/functional résumé, discussed in chapter 4 of this book.[4] Before you write your résumé, obtain samples from some individuals currently working in the field you wish to enter. These will give you a sense of the language and terminology of the professionals working in the field.

In stating your employment objective, put into your own words the nature of the position you are seeking, such as:

■ Executive director of a nonprofit human-service agency

Throughout your résumé, draw from both church and non-church sources in listing your skills and experiences. Try to draw from nonchurch sources for at least half of the items listed on your résumé. List your experience serving on community boards and agencies, for example, as well as previous secular work, especially work related to your objective. Remember to state your gifts and experience *in the language of the field you intend to enter.* For clergy aiming for a management position, your church experience, listed under "Professional Experience," would now be restated in "business" language, such as:

■ Organization and planning
■ Personnel supervision
■ Business management

When you have completed your résumé, have it critiqued by a professional currently employed in the field you wish to enter, and revise it in light of their comments.

Business Cards

Even though you are not yet employed in your new field, consider printing up some business cards listing you by your new profession. Business cards will help your in networking, and also in making contact with prospective employers.

Home Office

You need a specially designated work space to conduct your job search. If you are still employed in the church, you need to establish a separate home office. Having a specially designated space will encourage you to put in regular hours on your search, and also will provide a place for keeping files, receiving and returning messages, and performing other necessary functions relating to your search.

Networking

A major difficulty for clergy wishing to transition into secular work is that their current network is almost entirely in the church. Furthermore, the longer you have been *in* the church, the more true this is likely to be. Once you have committed yourself to seeking employment in a particular field, your next step is to build a network of contacts in that field. Resources for doing so include:

- parishioners and former church members employed in the field
- clergy who have transitioned into the field
- your previous informational interview contacts
- members of professional organizations in the field.

In order to research the names of professional organizations in the field, consult the *Occupational Outlook Handbook,* mentioned earlier, or the *Job Hunter's Sourcebook,* in your local library.[5]

The Interview

If you are serious about your intent to transfer into secular work, and you are conducting an organized, disciplined job search, it will not be long before you are interviewing for positions in your new field. Special issues matter to clergy who are interviewing for secular positions.

Two questions probably will be on the mind of your interviewers. The first is: Why is this person leaving the ministry? The second is: How is this person qualified for this position?

In terms of the first concern, your interviewers may have strong preconceptions about the church and "church people," which may make it difficult for them to perceive you simply as an individual with particular gifts to bring to this position. Your first task, therefore, during an interview, is to demonstrate, by word and manner, that you are simply a normal person and that you are able to relate to them, and to others, easily and effectively.

You may be asked, at some point, why you wish to leave the active ministry. Probably your best answer is simply to say that you have found most aspects of the ministry rewarding, but that you have found yourself increasingly drawn to the work and work environment of the position for which you are applying. In addition, stating that you and your family simply need more income than the active ministry provides is an argument that can be understood by most secular employers.

Your second task, as in any interview, is to demonstrate that you are qualified for the position. Let us assume that you are applying for a position as financial-aid officer of a local college. You would point out that financial management of the church is an important part of any minister's job. You would state that the ministry is a highly interpersonal profession and, therefore, that you relate easily to people, including young people of college age. You would say that parish ministry involves working with a variety of constituencies, a quality that would be important in this new position. Making these and other connections with your previous work, both in and outside the church, while focusing on the requirements of the prospective job, is your way of helping the interviewer perceive the "transferable skills" that you would bring to this new position.

Salary Negotiations

When you have been offered a new position, you enter a world unfamiliar to most clergy, one in which you are expected to bargain for top dollar in compensation.

The first thing to remember about salary negotiations is that they occur *after* you have definitely been offered a new position. Discussion about salary and benefits is unwise before this point. Second, in order to bargain effectively, you must know how much the position is worth. Check the latest edition of the *Occupational Outlook Handbook*, mentioned previously, and talk to friends and acquaintances working in the field. For helpful tips on salary negotiations, I recommend H. Anthony Medley's *Sweaty Palms: The Neglected Art of Being Interviewed.*[6]

EASING THE TRANSITION

The transition into secular work represents a major adjustment on the part of a former parish pastor. It profoundly affects the whole nature of your "self-image." In addition, it presents institutional and operational issues to deal with—new colleagues, a new work environment, a new focus of work. Finally, depending upon the circumstances of your leaving church employment, you may have strong residual emotions such as guilt, anger, or depression.

For these and other reasons, it is important to have sources of support, especially during the first few months of transition. This support may be drawn from former church colleagues, personal friends, career counselors, perhaps even your former judicatory executive. Clergy who have undergone the transition into secular work may prove the most helpful of all.

If your transition has been made for the right reasons, and you have been realistic in your expectations, you soon will find yourself enjoying the best of both the secular and the sacred worlds. In the secular world, you will find your contribution enormously enriched by your experience in the church. In the church, you now will be able to contribute as *you* see fit, determined by your own interests and abilities.

Many clergy who have made the transition into secular work believe that this combination is the best of all possible worlds.

Chapter Twelve

EPILOGUE

Abram and Sarai:
A Model for Clergy Transition

The LORD said to Abram . . . "I will make of you a great nation, and I will bless you . . . so that you will be a blessing."

Genesis 12:1*a*, 2*a*, *c*

The Old Testament story of Abram and Sarai, husband and wife, invokes a special fascination for those of us who are called by God and the Church into ministry.

Imagine the two of them sitting at the door of their tent in the cool of the evening, when the word of the Lord comes to them: "Go from your country and your kindred and your father's house to the land that I will show you. I will make of you a great nation . . . so that you will be a blessing."

What conflicted feelings they must have had! At first, undoubtedly shock and surprise. Later, probably a sense of apprehension at the thought of leaving behind all that was familiar and journeying forth into the unknown. Still later and ultimately, feelings of excitement and anticipation at the prospect of encountering new challenges and opportunities.

Abram and Sarai were experiencing feelings not unlike those of clergy and their families as they begin the search for a new call!

Like Abram, we too are called to journey forth at various stages in our careers. Like Abram, we may feel an initial resistance at the prospect of disrupting our lives and those of our families. Finally, like Abram, we experience a sense of excitement and anticipation as we face the challenges that a new call will bring.

The second major theme of the Abram story is the Lord's promise. Abram and Sarai will become parents of a great nation, and therefore a "blessing" to others. The Lord's promise to us results in a similar sense of becoming a "blessing" to others. If we invite God to become an active partner in our search; if we engage in the search in a spirit of true discernment; if, at the end, the church reaffirms our ordination, we

149

select wisely, and are chosen for our next call, then we indeed become a "blessing." We find ourselves in a new situation where we are challenged and stretched, and where our gifts find new expression in ministry to others.

Seeking a call to a new church, or even pursuing alternative forms of ministry is much more than simply a mechanical act of entering into the "placement process" or being "nominated" for an appointment. It is nothing less than a journey of faith—a journey that is, at the same time, frightening, challenging, and exhilarating, but one that promises blessings to us and to all those to whom we minister along the way.

Appendix A

METHODS OF CLERGY PLACEMENT IN SELECTED MAJOR DENOMINATIONS

The following is a summary of methods of clergy placement in 19 of the largest U.S. Protestant denominations, comprising approximately 50 million church members and more then 250,000 clergy. Listed for each denomination is the total number of churches, total membership, including the percentage of growth or decline since 1980, and the total number of clergy, including the percentage serving in parochial positions.[1] Also listed is the average salary for full-time pastors who are actively participating in the pension plan of the denomination.[2]

The relative degree of competition for parochial positions in each of the denominations is indicated by two figures. First, the percentage of membership growth or decline since 1980 suggests whether the total number of ministerial positions in the denomination is increasing or decreasing. Second, the percentage of ordained clergy serving in parochial positions indicates the proportion of clergy forced to seek positions outside parochial ministry.

A third factor to consider in any denomination is the average age of the clergy—over 50 in several denominations. For example, between 1988 and 2000, one-half of United Methodist clergy are expected to retire. This kind of transition may open up more positions for younger entrants, but it also puts enormous strain on pension plans. Such strain is further pressured by the number of second-career clergy in training at theological seminaries, where the average age may hover between 32 and 40.

The placement method classification[3] listed for each denomination includes one of the following:

• OPEN

The pastor takes the initiative in seeking a new call. The congregation exercises full autonomy in determining whom it will choose.

• RESTRICTED OPEN

The pastor exercises some degree of initiative and the congregation exercises some degree of autonomy. The judicatory sets standards of eligibility for clergy being considered for positions and may exercise approval of the final candidate.

• CLOSED

Pastors are assigned to churches by the bishop or equivalent judicatory head. Clergy and congregations do not exercise autonomy in placement. Any closed system also will include a significant number of mid-sized to large churches which quietly operate as if the system is open but restricted. And staff positions for associates or in program areas such as Christian education or youth ministry are pursued within a less regulated, open or restricted open system.

Information regarding placement procedures and resources has been provided by senior officials or by active clergy of each denomination. Placement procedures are written in the language and terminology of the denomination. Individual clergy are referred to as *they,* in accordance with the style used throughout the book, except in the case of denominations that ordain men only.

Printed materials available from national denominational headquarters and/or other widely circulated related materials are listed under Resources. In addition to these, individual synods, conferences, and dioceses may have printed materials available for clergy serving in their own jurisdiction.

DENOMINATIONS

African Methodist Episcopal Church

1134 Eleventh St. NW
Washington DC 20000
Churches: 8,000
Membership: 3,500,000*
Clergy (M/F): (Not Reported)
Salary: $10,000

Placement: Closed. The AME Church follows an appointive system. Pastors hear of openings from their bishop or through their network in the church. Pastors who want a transfer to a new congregation communicate this desire to their own bishop, or to the bishop of a district they would like to enter. Clergy are not allowed to take the initiative in approaching potential churches on their own. The bishop considers the needs of the congregation and the gifts of the pastor in making the appointment. Typically, the congregation and the pastor have not met each other prior to the bishop's announcement of the new appointment at the yearly conference meeting, although, in some circumstances, the bishop may inform the congregation of the appointment prior to the conference meeting.

*1991 figures

African Methodist Episcopal Zion Church

Department of Records and Research
P.O. Box 32843
Charlotte, NC 28232 (704)332-3851
Churches: 3,000*

Membership: 1,200,000*
Clergy (M/F): 2,686 (93% parochial)
Salary: (Not Reported)

Placement: Closed. The bishop exercises "Godly judgment" in making reappointments within each conference. Pastors wishing to be considered for reappointment hear of openings in their own conference and also throughout the country through their network in the church. If pastors wish to be reappointed within their own conference, they inform the presiding elder of their district, who, in turn, informs the bishop of the conference. If pastors wish to be considered for a pastoral appointment in another conference, they may contact the presiding elder of the district they wish to enter, or speak to the bishop of the conference and request a transfer from their own bishop. However, clergy may not directly contact a potential church. Conference bishops may meet periodically with presiding elders to discuss appointments and reappointments, and bishops informally discuss possible appointments whenever they meet. Reappointments are typically made quickly. Pastors do not interview, preach trial sermons, or otherwise meet with members of a prospective church. Congregations state leadership preferences to the bishop, and presiding elders offer recommendations, but the final decisions are made by the bishop. Appointments are announced each year at the Conference's Annual Session.
*1991 figures

American Baptist Churches in the U.S.A.

P.O. Box 851
Valley Forge, PA 19482 (610)768-2000
Churches: 5,845*
Membership: 1,534,078*
Clergy (M/F): 7,515 (60% parochial)
Salary: $31,725

Placement: Open. Professional Church Leaders (PCLs) learn of opportunities for serving through regional executive staff and from the *Ministry Opportunities Listing* (see Resources). PCLS wishing to relocate enroll in or update their American Baptist Personnel Services (ABPS) Profile. This is their ABC professional document created in Valley Forge for circulation in all regions. Profiles are matched with search requests from local churches or other AB related organizations through a computerized process. In addition, PCLs write to and/or call regional staff who are working with search committees to express interest in being considered for ministry positions. PCLs do not go directly to the churches. Profiles are given to search committees by regional staff. The search committee may select from the many Profiles three or four persons they wish to contact for further consideration. Persons selected are invited to interview and may also be visited in their own congregations. One PCL is selected as the candidate and invited to spend a weekend at the church. In advance of this visit and if all goes well during the visit, both the candidate and the church are expected to be reasonably committed to one another. On Sunday, after worship, or as specified in their constitution, the congregation votes to call by a unanimous or near unanimous vote. A letter of agreement has been drawn up in advance and this is approved. There is no approval required from the regional staff.

Resources: The Ministry Opportunities Listing, available by subscription to American Baptists only, is a monthly listing which includes openings both within ABC and ecumenical settings. Two brochures, "How Can I Move?" and "The Interview" give an overview of the American Baptist selection process. The "Suggested Minister-Church Agreement" provides a model for decisions made between the pastor and congregation. This is found in *Calling an American Baptist Minister,* which has been developed to assist search committees in the selection process. This manual, brochures, and other materials are available through American Baptist Personnel Services or the Commission on the Ministry, P.O. Box 851, Valley Forge, PA 19482-0851.
*1992 figures

Assemblies of God

1445 Boonville Avenue
Springfield, MO 65802 (417)862-2781
Churches: 11,689*
Membership: 2,257,846 (112% increase)
Clergy (M/F): 30,893* (56% parochial)
Salary: (Not Reported)

Placement: Open. Ministers hear of available positions through their network or from their district superintendent or the district superintendent of a district they would like to enter. Ordinarily, they make their résumé available to the district superintendent, who, in turn, presents it to the board of a church seeking a pastor, the board functioning as a pulpit committee. Ministers may also take the initiative in directly contacting available churches in their own or another district. A church board may also take the initiative in contacting a minister as to their availability to candidate, even though they may not have indicated they are open to making a change. A board may have under consideration a number of possible candidates, but an order of approach is usually established so that only one candidate is voted on at a time. There may be occasions when a candidate who is being considered by a church will be visited in their own church by the pulpit committee or representatives of it. They may then be invited to visit the potential church for a weekend to conduct Sunday services and meet the people. The final selection is made by

a two-thirds vote of the congregation in a duly called meeting. The congregation's selection does not have to be approved by the judicatory.
*1992 figures

Christian Church (Disciples of Christ)

222 South Downey Avenue
P.O. Box 1986
Indianapolis, IN 46206-1986 (317)353-1491
Churches: 3,996*
Membership: 1,011,502* (14% decline)
Clergy (M/F): 7,018 (55% parochial)
Salary: $30,788

Placement: Open. Regional and Area Ministers in each of the church's 35 regions provide advice and consent to both clergy and congregations. A minister wanting to relocate hears about seeking congregations from the Regional or Area Minister of the region they would like to enter. The minister updates the Ministerial Record Form, kept on file in the Division of Homeland Ministries, Center for Leadership & Ministry, in Indianapolis. The relocation file is mailed to all regional offices. The minister requests the Regional/Area Minister to submit their name to one or more seeking congregations of the region. Ministers are not to approach congregations on their own. The Regional/Area Ministers send each congregation a list of up to a dozen names for consideration. The search committee screens the names down to four or five, with the advice and counsel of the Regional/Area Minister of the region. Two or three candidates may be invited to the church to interview. Of these, one is selected as the candidate with whom to negotiate. Upon a positive vote of the church board, the congregation votes to call. A near unanimous or high majority vote is required, as mandated by the bylaws of the particular congregation. No ratification by the judicatory is required.

Resources: Relocation guidelines are described in a booklet, "Policies and Criteria for the Order of Ministry: Christian Church (Disciples of Christ)," published by the Center for Leadership and Ministry, Division of Homeland Ministries, and available from their office in Indianapolis, or from local regional offices. In addition, practical guidelines for ministers seeking relocation are contained in two booklets, "How Does the Relocation Process Work?" and "How to Help the Process Along."
*1992 figures

Church of God (Cleveland, Tennessee)

P.O. Box 2430
Cleveland, TN 37320 (615)472-3361

APPENDIX A

Churches: 5,776*
Membership: 672,008* (54% increase)
Clergy (M**): 6,898* (33% parochial)
Salary: $26,624

Placement: Closed. Pastoral appointments are made by the overseer before going to meet with the local congregation concerning the filling of a pastoral opening and/or the relocation of the present pastor. The overseer usually will present to a local church his recommendation(s) for pastor. Often the overseer will allow the congregation to cast a secret ballot concerning the recommendation(s). The overseer will then take the vote into consideration and will appoint the pastor of their choice, if possible. Any Church of God minister who hears of an opening in a church may ask the overseer for consideration as a nominee/recommendation to the congregation. Sometimes the local church council will request an interview with the nominees. It is not considered appropriate for ministers to directly contact local church members in order to seek support for selection. In the selection process, the overseer may recommmend one name or several. The overseer will seek the best choice for the church and will do everything possible to see that they feel positive about the newly appointed pastor. Whenever a minister is serving as a pastor and wishes to relocate, the overseer will try to select a replacement who will open a pastoral position so that each pastor has a place to serve. Completing a pastoral change is usually accomplished within two weeks to one month. The retirement of some pastors gives opportunity for new ministers to secure an appointment. New ministers are also often selected to plant a new congregation, with the help and support of the denomination.
*1992 figures
** Women are licensed and often appointed to pastor with full rights and authorities of a licensed minister. They are not eligible for ordained rank or for appointment as an overseer.

Church of the Nazarene

6401 The Paseo
Kansas City, MO 64131 (816)333-7000
Churches: 5,172*
Membership: 573,834* (18% increase)
Clergy (M/F): 9,363* (47% parochial)
Salary: $24,970

Placement: Restricted Open. Clergy work through district superintendents to secure a new position. They hear about available positions from their district superintendent or through their network in the church. Clergy wishing to move inform their district superintendent or that of a district they wish to enter, and update their placement materials on file in the district superinten-

dent's office. If they wish to leave the district, they may request that their name be shared informally with other judicatory executives at a meeting of the local Educational Region, comprising 10 to 15 districts. Clergy may not, however, take the initiative in approaching available churches on their own. When a vacancy occurs, the district superintendent provides the church with a list of qualified candidates. A small church may be appointed a pastor. A larger church may consider three or even more candidates. Candidates are visited and interviewed in their home congregation and preach a trial sermon. After all candidates have been considered, the board presents one name to the congregation, which selects on the basis of a two-thirds vote. The congregation's selection is then ratified by the district superintendent.
*1991 figures

Churches of Christ

No national headquarters.
Churches: 13,174
Membership: 1,684,872
Clergy (M**): (Not Reported)
Salary: (Not Reported)

Placement: Open. Clergy hear about openings through their network, from lists maintained by Christian universities, or from church periodicals (see Resources below). Churches may contact potential candidates directly and clergy may exercise great initiative in contacting available congregations. Informal connections are made at national spiritual renewal conferences, such as one held annually in Tulsa, Oklahoma, and at lectureships at Christian universities. The elders of a congregation, or their designated search committee, are charged with conducting the search. Potential candidates are visited in their home congregation. The list of candidates is narrowed to four or five, who are invited to spend a weekend at the church, meeting the congregation. One of these candidates is recommended by the search committee to the board of elders, who make the final determination. No congregational vote is necessary. Ratification by the judicatory is not required.

Resources: Churches list vacant positions and clergy may list their availability in the three major denominational publications: *Image Magazine, Gospel Advocate,* and *How Firm a Foundation.* Lists of vacant churches are maintained by Christian universities.
*1992 figures
** Women ministers are opposed by some on doctrinal grounds, but may be called by individual congregations.

The Episcopal Church

Episcopal Church Center
815 Second Avenue
New York, NY 10017 (212) 867-8400
Churches: 7,367*
Membership: 2,471,880* (11% decline)
Clergy (M/F): 14,878* (54% parochial)
Salary: $40,929

Placement: Restricted Open. A priest wishing to relocate works directly with their diocesan deployment officer and/or bishop. The priest updates their CDO (Church Deployment Office) profile, which is sent to New York and then computer matched with print-outs from available churches throughout the country. If a priest wishes to be considered for positions out of their home diocese, they contact the deployment officer and/or bishop of the diocese(s) they wish to enter. They may also request that their diocesan deployment officer share their availability at a Vacancy Sharing Consultation, held in various sections of the country. Depending upon the deployment procedures of the individual diocese, the priest may make direct personal contact with an available church, or work actively with the deployment officer of that diocese. The call is issued by the vestry at the recommendation of the search committee. The bishop of the diocese gives final approval to the call.

Resources: The CDO Office in New York, at the address above, publishes a monthly *Positions Open Bulletin,* listing positions across the country, available by subscription. The Vacancy Sharing Consultation of the province in which the priest is located may publish a newsletter listing available positions. In addition, the CDO Office publishes a variety of brochures to assist parishes and priests in the calling process. Among these are "More Than Fine Gold," a guide for preparing the CDO profile, and "Clergy Side of Interviewing in the Calling Process."
*1991 figures

Evangelical Lutheran Church in America

8767 West Higgins Road
Chicago, IL 60631 (312) 380-2700
Churches: 11,055*
Membership: (5,234,568*)** (3% decline)
Clergy (M/F): 17,416* (57% parochial)
Salary: $36,417

Placement: Restricted Open. Pastors and congregations work through synod bishops and their staff to effectuate pastoral changes. Pastors seeking new calls hear of openings from their own bishop or from the bishop of each synod they would like to enter. A Mobility Packet is completed by interested pastors and forwarded to the bishop. If they want to be considered out of the area, they request that the mobility form be distributed to additional synods. Pastors can also request their bishop to discuss their name and availability at a Mobility Consultation, a periodic regional meeting of bishops and staff of several synods. Pastors are discouraged from approaching individual congregations on their own, and congregations are expected to work through the synod office when seeking a new pastor. Congregations normally conduct a self-study and develop a profile of needed gifts in new pastoral leadership. The synod bishop and staff normally recommend 3 to 5 candidates to a congregation; in a few ELCA synods, only one candidate is submitted at a time. When pastors are being considered by a congregation, they may be phoned for a conference call interview. If selected as one of the final candidates, they are asked to interview with the congregation's call committee. Candidates usually are not asked to conduct a Sunday service or preach a trial sermon as part of the process. Following interviews, the call committee normally will recommend one candidate to the congregation. The congregation will decide by a two-thirds vote. Their selection must be attested by the bishop of the synod in which the congregation is located. After acceptance of the call, the pastor is installed in office by the bishop or the bishop's appointed representative.

*1992 figures

**Composite figure (see note 1, Appendix A)

The Lutheran Church—Missouri Synod

International Center
1333 South Kirkwood Road
St. Louis, MO 63122 (314)965-9000
Churches: 5,369*
Membership: 2,609,905* (1% decline)
Clergy (M): 8,799* (64% parochial)
Salary: $34,493

Placement: Restricted Open. Pastors wishing to move work through district presidents, who have the responsibility of making lists of suitable candidates available to a calling congregation. A pastor may also wish to suggest to his own or another district president that his name be placed on such call lists. His name may also be submitted by a member of the church's congregation. He himself, however, may not take the initiative in submitting his name to a potential congregation. The church's call committee will consider perhaps a dozen names consisting of those supplied by the district president and those submitted from outside. Of these, three or four finalists may be suggested to the voting membership of the congregation by a call committee. A small but increasing number of Missouri Synod congregations are utilizing an inter-

view-like process in selecting their final candidate. However, clergy being considered are typically not paid official, unannounced visits in their home congregations or expected to conduct a service or preach a trial sermon in the prospective church. Of the finalists, one may be recommended by the call committee to be approved by the congregation. However, the congregation makes the final decision. No judicatory approval is required, although the advice of the circuit counselor is typically sought.
*1992 figures

Presbyterian Church in America

1852 Century Place
Atlanta, GA 30345 (404)320-3366
Churches: 1,212
Membership: 239,500*
Clergy (M): 2,217 (62% parochial)
Salary: $34,667

Placement: Open. A minister wishing to move hears of vacant churches through his network or by reading the Vacant Church List, published by the Stated Clerk's Office in Atlanta (see below). He completes a form which summarizes his personal history, doctrinal positions and ministry priorities, known as a Ministerial Data Form, which is mailed to the office of the Stated Clerk. There it is matched with similar profiles of vacant churches. The minister can request that his profile be mailed to prospective churches by the Stated Clerk's Office or he can mail it himself. He can also request the profiles of churches he is interested in. The church's pastor search process typically begins with screening of the data forms, followed by a phone interview to the candidate from the search committee of the prospective church. This is usually followed by a visit of the pulpit committee to his present church to hear him preach, interview him further and meet his family. When the pulpit committee has narrowed the selection to one candidate, this candidate is invited to visit the church for more in-depth interviews, to meet the congregation, and to preach his candidating sermon. The selection is ratified by a majority vote of the congregation and must be approved by the presbytery to be final.

Resources: The Vacant Church List, available free, by request, from the Stated Clerk's office in Atlanta, lists available positions across the country. The rights and duties of ministers in the PCA regarding candidating procedures are spelled out in the Book of Church Order.
*1992 figures

Presbyterian Church (U.S.A.)

100 Witherspoon Street
Louisville, KY 40202 (502) 569-5000
Churches: 11,456*
Membership: (3,758,085*)** (12% increase)
Clergy (M/F): 20,527* (49% parochial)
Salary: $34,564

Placement: Restricted Open. Pastors hear about available openings by reading the *Opportunity List* (see Resources). A pastor wanting to seek a new call completes a Personal Information Form, and mails it to Call Referral Services in Louisville. In addition, Presbyterian pastors have the opportunity to meet members of pastor nominating committees of churches looking for new pastors at regional "Face-to-Face" events, held periodically around the country. Churches with vacancies complete a Church Information Form, which, after approval by the presbytery, is forwarded to Louisville for inclusion in the *Opportunity List,* as well as for computer matching and referral. When the pastor nominating committee has selected a pastor, procedures are followed in extending the call as outlined in the Book of Order.

Resources: The Presbyterian Church (U.S.A.) probably has developed the most comprehensive set of placement materials of any denomination. Positions are listed in *Opportunity List,* available upon request, according to the geographic area in which they are located. Lists also exist for specialized ministries, Christian education positions, and positions of special interest to racial/ethnic ministers. Placement related publications, available from the Vocation Agency in Louisville, include "TIPS for Clergy Seeking Relocation," "Seeking Your First Call," "Interviewing," and other publications on specialized topics.
*1992 figures
**Composite figure (see footnote 1, Appendix A)

Reformed Church in America

475 Riverside Drive, Room 1808
New York, NY 10115 (212) 870-2841
Churches: 927*
Membership: 274,521* (21% decline)
Clergy (M/F): 1,670* (56% parochial)
Salary: $39,737

Placement: Restricted Open. Ministers hear of openings from synod executives, from their network in the church, or from the *Opportunity List* (see Resources below). A pastor wishing to move updates the Minister's Profile and mails it to the church's Office of Ministry and Personnel Services in New York, where it is screened by denominational placement staff and matched with the profiles of open congregations, and also contacts synod executives of synods in which they would like to be considered. They could also request their synod executive to share their name with other synod executives at national meetings held two or three times a year. Ministers may approach available churches on their own, but are advised to do so through the congregation's supervising minister. A church typically will consider 20 to 40 candidates, most of these being recommended by the Office of Ministry and Personnel Services in New York or by synod executives. When a minister is being considered, the search committee will visit them in their home church and subsequently hear them preach at a neutral location or in their home congregation. Often, an interview in person or by speaker phone with the search committee precedes this step. Following hearing a candidate preach, the search committee narrows the selection to one candidate, who is invited by the consistory to lead worship at the open congregation. On the evening of the pastor's visit or shortly after, the congregation votes on their candidacy. This is an advisory vote, intended to "learn the mind of the congregation" and needs to be unanimous or near unanimous in order for the consistory of the church to make the final decision to call. The call is then approved on the judicatory level by the classis.

Resources: The *Opportunity List,* available by request from the Office of Ministry and Personnel Services in New York, lists open congregations by synod. More detailed information on individual churches is available from staff in New York, as well as from individual synod executives. The Reformed Church magazine, *The Church Herald,* sometimes contains classified ads for congregations looking for a minister.
*1992 figures

Seventh-day Adventist Church

12501 Old Columbia Pike
Silver Spring, MD 20904-6600 (301)680-6000
Churches: 4,261*
Membership: 748,687* (31% increase)
Clergy (M**): 4,355* (54% parochial)
Salary: $31,644

Placement: Restricted Open. A pastor hears about openings from the conference president and/or the ministerial director in his own or another conference, and from his network in the church. A pastor wishing to move within his own conference would so inform the conference president, who might give him a sense of which available churches would seem to be suitable for his gifts. If a pastor wanted to be considered out of the area, he would request the local president to contact the president of the conference in which he wished to be considered, or would contact this person directly, requesting that he inform his own conference president. A pastor may also take the initiative in contacting potential churches on his own. After a church has received a list of potential candidates, they will screen the list down to several finalists who might be interviewed by the head elder and the church board and/or board of elders. A congregational vote is not required, but a candidate may request to appear before the business meeting of the whole church, and perhaps have a "straw vote" taken on his candidacy, as a precondition for accepting the call. The conference president, empowered by the executive committee of the conference, issues the official call.

Resources: Practical, "how to" articles on aspects of the ordained ministry, including placement, are printed in *Ministry,* a magazine of the Seventh-day Adventist Church.

*1992 figures

** Women are not ordained, but may be licensed to serve as fully functioning pastors of congregations.

Southern Baptist Convention

901 Commerce Street, Suite 750
Nashville, TN 37203 (615) 244-2355
Churches: 38,401*
Membership: 15,358,866* (13% increase)
Clergy (M/F**): 63,352* (61% parochial)
Salary: (Not Reported)

Placement: Open. Pastors wanting to move hear of openings through their network in the church or by speaking to the Director of Missions of the district association and of the state board of the area in which they would like to be considered. Pastors may supply biographical information to be kept on file in the office of Church Minister Relations of their state board. Southern Baptist pastors exercise great initiative in making their availability known to prospective congregations, although they may prefer to have a third party contact a church directly on their behalf. After receiving a preliminary inquiry from a pastor search or personnel committee of a prospective church, the pastor sends résumés, sermon tapes, and other relevant materials. After receiving materials from several candidates, the search committee will identify one or more candidates to be visited in their home congregation and possibly interviewed after the service. Of these, one will be selected. This candidate is then invited to spend a period of time, perhaps a weekend, or at least a Sunday, at the church. The candidate preaches and meets with church members and groups. Following the Sunday service, and upon recommendation of the search committee, the congregation votes to call by a majority or by a two-thirds vote, although individual pastors and also congregations may require greater unanimity as a precondition of finalizing a call. No judicatory approval is necessary.

Resources: Individual state conventions have developed printed resources to assist in the calling of a pastor. The Baptist General Association of Virginia has developed a particularly complete selection of resources, which are available to pastors and congregations outside the area, upon request, by calling (804) 672-2100. Denominational magazines sometimes list specialized positions in the church. The core Southern Baptist Convention seminaries have developed placement resources for recent graduates, which are also available to pastors in the field, upon request.

*1992 figures

**The Southern Baptist Convention does not encourage the ordination of women, although a small number of women have been called as pastors in the denomination. The decision to call is made by the individual congregation.

Unitarian Universalist Association

25 Beacon Street
Boston, MA 02108 (617)742-2100
Churches: 1,037*
Membership: 149,592*
Clergy (M/F): 1,236* (63% parochial)
Salary: (Not Reported)

Placement: Restricted Open. Ministers and congregations work through the Ministerial Settlement Director to effectuate a new call. Ministers hear about openings through their network or by reading *Opportunities for Ministry* (see Resources). A minister interested in moving updates the Ministerial Record Sheet, kept on file at the Ministerial Settlement Office in Boston, and indicates what congregations they are interested in being considered for. Ministers do not approach congregations on their own, but do have the right to have their materials sent to any congregation in which they are interested, if they hold appropriate U.U.A. credentials. The Ministerial Settlement Director sends an initial list of approximately a dozen potential candidates to a vacant congregation, and may subsequently send a supplementary list of additional candidates. Upon receipt of the list, the congregation sends a packet of information to all ministers on the list. Ministers interested in being considered respond by sending their packet of information to the church. The search committee selects three or four precandidates who are invited to spend a weekend privately with the committee, including leading worship at a nearby church. The search committee reaches consensus on one candidate. This person is invited to the congregation for candidating week, a period of eight days, including two consecutive Sundays. After the second Sunday, the congregation votes to call and approves the contract by a unanimous or near unanimous vote. The congregational vote does not need to be ratified by the judicatory.

Resources: "Opportunities for Ministry" appears in *The World,* the denominational magazine, and is also mailed periodically to all clergy. The *Ministerial Settlement Manual for Ministers,* given to all seminarians at graduation, describes settlement procedures. A book by Peter Spilman Raible, titled *How to Case a Church: An Irreverent Guide to Finding and Getting the Church of Your Choice,* assists ministers in interpreting church data and provides an overview of the settlement process.

*1993 figures
**Composite figure (see note 1, Appendix A)

United Church of Christ

700 Prospect Avenue
Cleveland, OH 44115 (216)736-2100
Churches: 6,264
Membership: 1,555,382 (10% decline)
Clergy (M/F): 10,203 (44% parochial)
Salary: $31,335

Placement: Open. Ministers hear about available openings from conference staff who serve as placement ministers or by reading *United Church Employment Opportunities* (see Resources). A minister wanting to move completes or updates the Ministerial Profile kept on file at the Office for Church Life and Leadership in Cleveland. The minister requests that their Profile be mailed to the placement minister in areas where they would like to be considered. Ministers seeking a new setting for ministry do not approach a vacant congregation directly, but rather through the designated placement minister. Ministers can increase visibility by having their name listed in the monthly *Persons Seeking New Opportunities* (see Resources). Congregational search committees typically will screen down to three or four prefinalists, who are interviewed and may preach in a neutral pulpit. One finalist is selected whose call is affirmed at a congregational meeting by a high majority vote, usually following a "candidating" or "trial" sermon to the congregation. No judicatory ratification is necessary.

Resources: "When A Pastor Seeks a New Place for Ministry" gives procedural guidelines for ministers seeking new positions. *United Church Employment Opportunities,* available by subscription, is a monthly listing of church positions, agency positions, and some ecumenical and overseas positions. A minister seeking a call may choose to be listed in *Persons Seeking New Opportunities,* a confidential listing sent to agency executives and placement ministers. Listings are carried for six months, but can be renewed. A request for subscriptions, publications, and available listings are made through the Office for Church Life and Leadership in Cleveland.

*1992 figures

**Composite figure (see note 1, Appendix A)

The United Methodist Church

No national headquarters.
Churches: 37,100*
Membership: 8,789,101* (8% decline)
Clergy (M/F): 38,492* (53% parochial)
Salary: $34,832

Placement: Closed. The United Methodist Church, and other churches of the United Methodist tradition, are distinctive in American Protestantism in following an appointive rather than a call system. Most clergy move within their own Annual Conference. Pastors desiring a new appointment inform the District Superintendent of the Conference at the time of their annual consultation, generally held around the first of the year. If a pastor is to be reappointed, the decision is usually made in February or March, and the move occurs in June. The District Superintendent, after consulting with the pastor and with the Pastor-Parish Relations Committee of a church, presents the name of a potential appointee to the Cabinet of the Annual Conference for approval. Following this, the Pastor-Parish Relations Committee of a congregation is notified. The pastor meets with the members of the committee following the notification, although some conferences schedule this meeting to occur prior to the approval of the Cabinet. Unless serious reservations are expressed by either the pastor, or by members of the Pastor-Parish Relations Committee, the appointment is finalized by the conference bishop through the Cabinet.

Resources: Who Will Go for Us?: An Invitation to Ordained Ministry, by Dennis Campbell (Abingdon Press, 1994). *The Episcopal Leadership Role in United Methodism,* by Roy H. Short (Abingdon Press, 1985). For persons who wish to explore ordination in The United Methodist Church, applications and materials are available from The General Board of Higher Education and Ministry, Division of Ordained Ministry, United Methodist Center, Nashville, TN 37202.

*1991 figures

Appendix B

SEARCH PROCESS CHECKLIST

This checklist is based on a two-year timeline, from beginning your search to receiving a new call or appointment. Year One is a time of preparation. Unless they are seeking appointment beyond the local church, clergy who work in closed systems are likely to complete their efforts within the first year. Year Two is the time of the search itself. For a more detailed discussion of each step, the reader is referred to the chapters indicated.

GETTING READY FOR YOUR SEARCH

(Time: Approximately one year)

1. Make an intentional decision either to stay in your present ministry or to seek a new call (see chapter 2).
2. Clearly identify the type of ministry to which you feel called (see chapter 2).
3. Inform denominational officials that you would like to be considered for a new call.
4. Prepare placement materials (see chapter 4).

THE SEARCH

(Time: One year, from beginning your search to receiving a new call.)

The Beginning

(See chapter 5.)

1. Investigate all channels for learning about vacancies. Subscribe to the Positions Open Bulletin, if such a publication exists in your denomination.
2. Indicate your availability to prospective churches, in accordance with the placement procedures used in your denomination (see appendix A).
3. Build a support group to assist you.
4. Schedule a regular weekly time for search-related tasks.
5. Continue to respond to prospective churches and to generate new possibilities.
6. Remain emotionally involved with your present ministry.

Candidating

(See chapter 7, except as noted.)

1. Prepare yourself mentally, physically, and spiritually.
2. Finalize all arrangements for your scheduled visit.

3. Review all church materials, as well as your own ministerial records (see chapter 6).

4. Research the community in which the church is located (see chapter 6).

5. Review the questions they are likely to ask, as well as the concerns you want to share with them.

6. Consider preparing a Contributions Document (see chapter 4).

7. Write your candidating sermon.

8. While at the church, conduct an effective interview, using the "T-BAR Technique."

9. After your return home, write thank-you notes to your hosts and to the other principals involved.

10. If offered the call, decide prayerfully, and in accordance with your personal and career goals, whether you will accept.

Contract and Salary Negotiations

(In some denominations this will occur as part of candidating week, or it will be taken from published ranges.)

(See chapter 8, except as noted.)

1. In advance of negotiations, list the salary and benefits you are currently receiving.

2. Request from your denominational office a sample Letter of Agreement and compensation guidelines.

3. Review all financial data from your prospective church.

4. Review your own financial, personal, career, and family goals. Decide, in advance of negotiations, which items in the Letter of Agreement are of particular importance to you and your family.

5. Determine whether you will have a denominational official or consultant to assist you in salary negotiations.

6. Review the principles of "win-win negotiating" before discussing salary and benefits with the church.

Transitioning

(See chapter 9.)

1. Give notice to your present church, allowing six to eight weeks before departure.

2. Participate willingly in a congregational farewell event, if planned.

3. Say your own personal good-byes to members of the congregation.

4. If you own your own house, put it on the market, and make an offer on a house in your new location.

5. Make arrangements with a mover. Complete all necessary relocation tasks (see checklist in chapter 7).

APPENDIX B

Starting a New Ministry

(See chapter 9.)

1. The first few days in your new church, note anything that seems strange or unusual.

2. Tell the congregation, by word and example, what you want them to know about you.

3. Early in your new ministry, call on members of your congregation. Encourage them to share their hopes, dreams, and concerns about the congregation.

4. Meet with the former pastor and come to an agreement about whether, and in what fashion, they will continue to participate in the life of the congregation.

5. Begin to establish yourself and your family in the life of the wider community.

6. Build a formal or informal support group to assist you in your new ministry.

7. Plan your institution.

8. Choose your first major initiative. Select it on the basis of congregational need, rather than your own personal preference. Do not institute major changes, especially in worship, during the first 12 to 18 months.

9. Work with your lay leaders to draft a mission goal statement, pointing the congregation toward future directions in ministry.

Appendix C

RESOURCES

The following items are basic resources for clergy seeking a new call, listed in the order in which you would access them as you conduct your search. I have listed the latest available edition for each.

GENERAL

Mastering Transitions, by Ed Bratcher, Robert Kemper, and Douglas Scott, a part of *Christianity Today's* Mastering Ministry series, discusses the practical as well as the emotional consequences of moving to a new church, with particular stress upon the start-up phase (Portland, Oreg.: Multnomah, 1991).

DEFINING YOUR MINISTRY

Your Next Pastorate: Starting the Search, by Richard N. Bolles, Russell C. Ayers, Arthur F. Miller, and Loren B. Mead, provides helpful exercises for identifying your gifts for ministry (An Alban Institute publication, No. AL122, 1990, available from the Institute: 4550 Montgomery Ave., Ste. 433 North, Bethesda MD 20814-3341. (Tel. 1-800-486-1318, Ext. 244)

The relationship of church size to pastoral-leadership style is explored by Lyle E. Shaller in *The Small Church Is Different; The Small Membership Church: Scenarios for Tomorrow; The Middle-Sized Church: Problems and Prescriptions; The Multiple Staff and the Larger Church;* and, on developing a mission congregation, *Growing Plans: Strategies to Increase Your Church's Membership.* You also cannot understand what is happening to smaller churches without reading about the affect of large institutions, such as *The Seven-Day-A-Week Church* (Nashville: Abingdon Press, 1982, 1994, 1985, 1980, 1983, and 1992, respectively).

Personality Type and Religious Leadership, by Roy M. Oswald and Otto Kroeger, analyzes styles of ministry based upon a knowledge of one's temperamental characteristics (Bethesda: Alban Institute, No. AL103, 1988).

J. Keith Cook and Lee C. Moorehead's *Six Stages of a Pastor's Life* helps to place career decisions in the context of the entire life-cycle (Nashville: Abingdon Press, 1990).

PLACEMENT MATERIALS

Probably the two best books on writing a résumé are Richard Lathrop's *Who's Hiring Who?* 12th ed., and Yana Parker's *The Damn Good Resume Guide,* rev. ed., both from Ten Speed Press, 1989. Although written for a secular audience, both books provide valuable insights about presenting oneself effectively on paper for any position, in or out of the church.

CANDIDATING

Mastering Transitions, by Ed Bratcher et al., mentioned previously, contains a succinct summary of the major issues that need to be addressed during the candidating interview.

Two excellent books on interviewing in general are Martin John Yate's *Knock 'Em Dead: The Ultimate Job Seeker's Handbook* (Holbrook, Mass.: Bob Adams, 1994), and the revised edition of *Sweaty Palms: The Neglected Art of Being Interviewed,* by H. Anthony Medley (Berkeley, Calif.: Ten Speed Press, 1992).

The community in which the church is located can be researched in Richard Boyer and David Savageau's *Places Rated Almanac: Your Guide to Finding the Best Places to Live in America,* rev. ed. (Englewood Cliffs, N.J.: Prentice Hall, 1993).

LETTER OF AGREEMENT

Resources include two books by Manfred Holck, Jr.: *Handbook of Personal Finance for Ministers* (Minneapolis: Augsburg Press, 1990), which presents a procedure for negotiating a pay package with a church, and *Housing for Clergy* (Ivergrove, Minn.: Logos, 1993), which discusses the relative advantages of a housing allowance and church-owned housing. Clergy performance evaluations are discussed in Roy M. Oswald's *Getting a Fix on Your Ministry* (Bethesda: Alban Institute, No. OD39).

TRANSITIONING

Running Through the Thistles: Terminating a Ministerial Relationship with a Parish, by Roy M. Oswald, will assist you in dealing effectively with issues surrounding the leaving of your present parish (Bethesda: Alban Institute, No. AL36, 1991). Another similar resource is Edward A. White's *Saying Goodbye: A Time of Growth for Congregations and Pastors,* which also contains a "farewell" worship service (Bethesda: Alban Institute, No. AL118, 1991).

When preparing for the move itself, a comprehensive resource is Carolyn Janik's *Positive Moves* (New York: Grove-Atlantic, 1988). For preparing small children for a move, I recommend *Moving,* written by TV's "Mr. Rogers" (Fred Rogers) (New York: G. P. Putnam's Sons, 1987).

When beginning your new position, succinct summaries of start-up issues can be found in Roy M. Oswald's *The Pastor as Newcomer* (Bethesda: Alban Institute No. AL18, 1990). *New Beginnings: Pastorate Start-up Workbook,* rev. ed., by the same author, presents step-by-step procedures for dealing with start-up issues (Bethesda: Alban Institute, No. AL111, 1992), Finally, John C. Fletcher's classic *Religious Authenticity in the Clergy* (Bethesda: Alban Institute, No. OD70, 1975), describes the process by which clergy are "authenticated" in a new congregation.

After you have settled in, Kent R. Hunter's *Your Church Has Personality* (Nashville: Abingdon Press, 1985) will help you understand the context in which any long-range ministry planning must take place; and Robert W. Johnson's *Being the Church* (Bethesda: Alban, No. OD32, 1981), provides a training format for such planning.

WOMEN CLERGY

A helpful resource for female clergy of all denominations is *Following the Call: Search Process Guidelines for Women in Ministry,* a brochure available from the Women in Ministry Office, American Baptist Churches—USA, P.O. Box 851, Valley Forge PA 19482 (Tel. 215-768-2000).

Women Clergy: Breaking Through Gender Barriers, by Edward C. Lehman, describes factors working for and against the placement of women in the church, and identifies effective strategies for seeking placement (New Brunswick, N.J.: Transaction Books, 1985).

For women seeking or accepting a call to a staff position, *The Male-Female Church Staff: Celebrating the Gifts, Confronting the Challenges,* by Anne Marie Neuchterlein and Celia Allison Hahn, provides insight on gender-related issues in the workplace (Bethesda: Alban Institute, No. AL119, 1993).

SPECIAL CIRCUMSTANCES

Your Next Pastorate: Starting the Search, by Richard N. Bolles et al., mentioned previously, contains special sections on dealing with imminent separation or dissolution of the pastoral contract, and also on clergy with disabilities (Bethesda: Alban Institute, No. AL122, 1989). Emily Koltnow and Lynne S. Dumas' *CONGRATULATIONS! You've Been Fired: Sound Advice for Women Who've Been Terminated, Pink-Slipped, Downsized, or Otherwise Unemployed,* provides practical help and advice for anyone who has been terminated (New York: [Columbine] Fawcett, 1990).

For women or men interested in interim ministry, Ralph Macy's *The Interim Pastor* describes the nature of this specialized ministry (Bethesda: Alban Institute, No. OD91, 1978).

SECULAR EMPLOYMENT

For clergy interested in exploring the possibility of secular employment, here are several helpful resources for self-assessment.

See especially the epilogue, "How to Find Your Mission in Life," in Richard Nelson Bolles' *What Color Is Your Parachute?* (Berkeley, Calif.: Ten Speed Press, revised annually).

What I REALLY Want to Do: How to Discover the Right Job, by Christopher Chamberlin Moore (St. Louis: CBP [Chalice] Press, 1989).

Wishcraft: How to Get What You Really Want, by Barbara Sher (New York: Ballantine Books, 1983).

Choosing Your Career, Finding Your Vocation: A Step-by-Step Guide for Adults and Counselors, by Roy Lewis, is particularly helpful for mid-life issues (Mahwah, N.J.: Paulist Press, 1989).

For specific information about particular occupations, the *Occupational Outlook Handbook,* a government publication revised every two years and available in the "Reference" section of your library, describes more than two hundred occupations, representing well over half of all the jobs in the United States.

When beginning your job search, Michelle Le Compte's *JOB HUNTER'S SOURCEBOOK: Where to find employment leads and other job search resources,* 2nd ed., provides sources of information and job leads for 155 different occupations (Detroit: Gale Research, 1992).

Finally, two of the best books for getting hired in the secular marketplace: *The Right Place at the Right Time: Finding a Job in the 1990s,* rev. ed., by Robert Wegmann and Robert Chapman (Berkeley, Calif.: Ten Speed Press, 1990).

Guerrilla Tactics in the New Job Market, 2nd ed., by Tom Jackson (New York: Bantam Books, 1991).

PASTORAL EVALUATION

Either while you are conducting self-assessment, or after you accept a new position, you may want to dig more deeply into the issues of *Clergy Assessment and Career Development,* edited by Richard A. Hunt, John Hinkle, Jr., and H. Newton Maloney (Nashville: Abingdon Press, 1990). While judicatory officials and seminary executives may be more interested in the psychological tools and statistics, you will get a much broader understanding of the national outlook for clergy deployment from these thirty-five essays. The book suggests several ways to go about annual ministry evaluations.

Appendix D

CHURCH CAREER DEVELOPMENT CENTERS

These following centers are accredited and coordinated by the Career Development Council, Room 861, 475 Riverside Dr., New York NY 10115; Tel. 212-870-2144. The Church Career Development Council (CCDC) was organized in 1969 to develop and accredit regional centers to provide specialized career counseling resources for persons in professional leadership positions in the church. Two programs are available:

1. The individual career counseling program is normally a two- or three-day consultation, during which a person works privately with the professional staff. This program is available throughout the year.

2. Special group career counseling programs are offered also by most of the centers.

The cost varies, depending upon judicatory membership in a center. For specific information on fees, consult the location closest to you.

Generally speaking, the service offered by the Church Career Development Centers tend to be stronger in assessment (i.e., determining where your strengths lie) than in "marketing" (helping you actually land a position). For the latter, you will need to rely primarily on your denominational placement officer, if it is a church related position, or on your own personal resources, if you are seeking secular work. (See the "Secular Employment" section under "Resources" in appendix C.)

The Midwest Career Development Service, with three locations, sponsors "Crossings," an outplacement program specifically designed for those wishing to transfer out of the church into secular employment.

ARLINGTON, TEXAS
  Southwest Career Development Center, P.O. Box 5923, Arlington TX 76005; Tel. 817-640-5181; the Reverend William M. Gould, Jr., Director.

ATLANTA, GEORGIA
  Career Development Center of the Southeast, 531 Kirk Rd., Decatur GA 30030; Tel. 404-371-0336; Dr. Robert M. Urie, Director.

BOSTON, MASSACHUSETTS
  Center for Career Development and Ministry, 70 Chase St., Newton Centre MA 02159; Tel. 617-969-7750; Dr. Stephen E. Ott, Director.

CHURCH CAREER DEVELOPMENT CENTERS

CHICAGO, ILLINOIS
Midwest Career Development Service, P.O. Box 7249, 1840 Westchester Blvd., Westchester IL 60154; Tel. 708-343-6268; Dr. L. Ronald Brushwyler, Executive Director.

COLUMBUS, OHIO
Midwest Career Development Service, 1520 Old Henderson Rd., #102B, Columbus OH 43220; Tel. 614-442-8822; the Reverend John R. Matthews, Associate Director for Columbus.

KANSAS CITY, KANSAS
Midwest Career Development Service, P.O. Box 2816, 754 N. 31st St., Kansas City KS 66110-0816; Tel. 913-621-6348; Sheryl C. Famcher, M.A., Associate Director for Kansas City.

LANCASTER, PENNSYLVANIA
Lancaster Career Development Center, 1401 Columbia Ave., Lancaster PA 17603; Tel. 717-397-7451; the Reverend L. Guy Mehl, Executive Director.

LAURINBURG, NORTH CAROLINA
Career and Personal Counseling Service, St. Andrew's Presbyterian College, 1700 Dogwood Mile, Laurinburg NC 28352; Tel. 910-276-3162; Dr. Elbert R. Patton, Director.

OAKLAND, CALIFORNIA
The Center for Ministry, 8393 Capwell Dr., #220, Oakland CA 94621-2123; Tel. 510-635-4246; Dr. Robert L. Charpentier, Director.

PRINCETON, NEW JERSEY
Northeast Career Center, 407 Nassau St., Princeton NJ 08540; Tel. 609-924-9408; Dr. Roy Lewis, Director.

ST. PAUL, MINNESOTA
North Central Career Development Center, 516 Mission House Lane, New Brighton MN 55112; Tel. 612-636-5120; Dr. Kenneth J. McFayden, Executive Director.

ST. PETERSBURG, FLORIDA
Career and Personal Counseling Center, Eckerd College, P.O. Box 12560, St. Petersburg FL 33733; Tel. 813-864-8356; the Reverend John Sims, Director.

For programs in Canada, contact Dr. Richard G. Johns; Tel. 604-537-2339.

175

NOTES

1. CLERGY PLACEMENT

1. The names given in this chapter are fictitious. The persons portrayed represent composites of many individuals in typical pastoral situations.

2. I have served as a deployment officer in the Episcopal diocese of New Jersey since 1990.

3. Richard Nelson Bolles, *What Color Is Your Parachute?* rev. ed. (Berkeley, Calif.: Ten Speed Press, 1989), p. 43.

2. WHEN TO SEEK A NEW BEGINNING

1. Barbara Sher, with Annie Gottlieb, *Wishcraft: How to Get What You Really Want* (New York: Ballantine Books, 1979), pp. 227-37.

3. YOUR MINISTRY, IN TWENTY-FIVE WORDS OR LESS

1. *Testing and Reclaiming Your Call to Ministry,* by Robert Schnase (Nashville: Abingdon Press, 1991) is helpful in discussing the concept of call within the context of the ordained ministry. Two books provide practical exercises for sharpening and defining your sense of call: *What I REALLY Want to Do: How to Discover the Right Job,* by Christopher Chamberlin Moore (St. Louis: CBP [Chalice] Press, 1989), and *Your Next Pastorate: Starting the Search,* by Richard N. Bolles, Russell C. Ayres, Arthur F. Miller, and Loren B. Mead (Washington, D.C.: The Alban Institute, 1990). For readers familiar with the Myers-Briggs Types Indicator, a book by Roy M. Oswald and Otto Kroeger, *Personality Type and Religious Leadership* (Washington, D.C.: The Alban Institute, 1988) provides valuable insight into one's preferred style of ministry, as rooted in the dynamic of one's temperament.

2. I am indebted to several authors in the field of career development and personal growth for the original ideas behind the exercises suggested in this chapter: Richard Nelson Bolles, *What Color Is Your*

Parachute? (Berkeley, Calif.: Ten Speed Press, revised annually), for "Things that bug me," and "A perfect day in the ministry"; Bernard Haldane, *Career Satisfaction and Success* (New York: AMACOM, 1978), for "My greatest achievements," suggested by his System to Identify Motivated Skills (SIMS), pp. 33-63; and Barbara Sher, with Annie Gottlieb, *Wishcraft: How to Get What You Really Want* (New York: Ballantine, 1979), for "Mentors and role models," suggested by "Creating your own cheering section," pp. 43-45.

3. For the first three categories, I draw upon the observations of Lyle E. Schaller in three of his books written for the Abingdon Press Creative Leadership Series: *The Small Church Is Different* (1982), *The Middle Sized Church: Problems and Prescriptions* (1985), and *The Multiple Staff and the Larger Church* (1980), all by Abingdon Press in Nashville. The characteristics of the fourth category, new church/mission developer, are drawn from *Growing Plans: Strategies to Increase Your Church's Membership,* also by Lyle Schaller (Nashville: Abingdon Press, 1983), pp. 135-38. In his recently published *The Seven-Day-A-Week Church* (Nashville: Abingdon Press, 1992), Schaller discusses the continuing trend toward bigness in American Protestantism during the past couple of decades. A somewhat different church-size typology is described by Arlin Rothauge in *Sizing Up a Congregation for a New Member Ministry* (The Episcopal Church Center, 815 Second Avenue, New York, 10017).

4. Author and church consultant Lyle E. Schaller originated the terminology "shepherd" and "rancher" to denote two very different pastoral styles. For an analysis of the two styles and their relation to church size, I recommend C. Peter Wagner's *Leading Your Church to Growth* (Ventura, Calif.: Regal Books, 1984).

5. If you sense the call to blue-collar ministry, read Tex Sample's *Hard Living People and Mainstream Christians* (Nashville: Abingdon Press, 1992) to get an excellent perspective on the needed gifts and graces. Two additional books also describe the distinctive characteristics of ministry to a blue-collar congregation: Sample's earlier book, *Blue-Collar Ministry* (Valley Forge, Penna: Judson Press, 1984) and Steele W. Martin with Priscilla C. Martin, *Blue-Collar Ministry* (Washington, D.C.: The Alban Institute, 1989).

4. PREPARING YOUR MATERIALS

1. Yana Parker, *The Damn Good Resume Guide,* rev. ed. (Berkeley, Calif.: Ten Speed Press, 1989).

5. IDENTIFYING VACANCIES

1. For the helpful distinctions involving the open, restricted open, and closed methods of deployment, I am indebted to Jackson W. Carroll and Robert L. Wilson, *Too Many Pastors? The Clergy Job Market* (New York: The Pilgrim Press, 1980), pp. 33-35.

2. Richard Nelson Bolles, *What Color Is Your Parachute?* (Berkeley, Calif.: Ten Speed Press, 1989), p. 44.

3. Ibid., p. 17.

4. Barbara Sher, with Annie Gottlieb, *Wishcraft: How to Get What You Really Want* (New York: Ballantine Books, 1979), pp. 227-37.

5. Bolles, *What Color Is Your Parachute?* p. 44.

6. "CASING" A CHURCH

1. The title of this chapter is based on a book by Unitarian Universalist Peter Spilman Raible, *How to Case a Church: An Irreverent Guide to Finding and Getting the Church of Your Choice,* 3rd ed. (Boston: Unitarian Universalist Minister's Association, 1987).

2. Called in various denominations the Church Information Form or the Congregational Profile.

3. David Savageau and Richard Boyer, *Places Rated Almanac: Your Guide to Finding the Best Places to Live in America,* rev. ed. (Englewood Cliffs, N.J.: Prentice Hall, 1993).

4. *Blue Collar Ministry: Problems and Opportunities in Mainline "Middle" Congregations,* by Steele W. Martin, with Priscilla C. Martin (Washington, D.C.: The Alban Institute, 1989); also *Blue Collar Ministry* (Valley Forge, Penna.: Judson Press, 1984) and *Hard Living People and Mainstream Christians* (Nashville: Abingdon Press, 1992), both by Tex Sample.

5. Kent R. Hunter, *Your Church Has Personality* (Nashville: Abingdon Press, 1985).

6. John David Webb, *How to Change the Image of Your Church* (Nashville: Abingdon Press, 1993).

7. Raible, *How to Case a Church*, p.32

7. THE CANDIDATING INTERVIEW

1. Probably the two best books on interviewing in general are Martin John Yates' *Knock 'Em Dead: The Ultimate Job Seekers' Handbook* (Holbrook, Mass.: Bob Adams, 1994), and *Sweaty Palms: The Neglected Art of Being Interviewed*, rev. ed., by H. Anthony Medley (Berkeley, Calif.: Ten Speed Press, 1992). *The Perfect Follow-up Method to Get the Job*, by Jeffrey Allen (New York: John Wiley & Sons, 1991) discusses follow-up techniques you can use *after* the interview.

2. John T. Malloy's *Dress for Success* (New York: Warner Books, 1976) discusses clothes and personal appearance, and their effect of how people perceive you. There is a companion volume by the same author: *The Woman's Dress for Success Book* (New York: Warner Books, 1978). In Malloy's *Live for Success* (New York: Bantam Books, 1983), this same author takes a broader perspective, looking not only at clothes but also at body language and speech patterns. You may not like what Malloy has to say, but you can't ignore it.

3. Roger Ailes, with John Krauchar, *You Are the Message* (New York: Doubleday, 1988).

4. The T-BAR technique, developed by Communespond, a management consultant firm specializing in providing training for corporate interviews, was profiled by Robert C. Anderson in "Fashion Your Future," *Success* (February 1986), p. 62.

5. *The Clergy Side of Interviewing in the Calling Process* (New York: Church Deployment Board of The Episcopal Church, 1985). The checklist in this pamphlet is adapted from *The Job Club Counselor's Manual*, by Nathan Azrin and Victoria A. Besalel (Baltimore: University Park Press, 1980).

8. LETTER OF AGREEMENT

1. Adapted from *How to Pay Your Pastor More and Balance the Budget Too*, by Manfred Holck, Jr. (Austin, Tex.: Church Management, Inc., 1988), p. 84, reissued by Logos Publications, Invergrove, MN.

2. Two books written by CPA Manfred Holck, Jr. are helpful resources for clergy who wish to build a compensation package with a church: *Handbook of Personal Finance for Ministers* (Minneapolis: Augsburg Press, 1990), which presents a procedure for negotiating a pay package with a church; and *Housing for Clergy* (Ivergrove, Minn.: Logos, 1993), which discusses the relative advantages of a housing allowance and church-owned housing.

3. Richard Nelson Bolles, *What Color Is Your Parachute?* (Berkeley, Calif.: Ten Speed Press, 1990), p. 338.

4. For a more detailed analysis of current IRS regulations regarding clergy compensation, beyond the scope of this book, the reader is referred to the *Abingdon Clergy Income Tax Guide*, revised and updated every year by Deloitte & Touche, and also available by subscription. (Order Toll Free 1-800-672-1789 or mail to Cokesbury Subscriptions, P.O. Box 801, Nashville TN 37202.)

5. Holck, in *Housing for Clergy*, describes how selling the parsonage and using the proceeds to establish a housing allowance can cost no more than keeping the parsonage, and has the additional advantage of providing significant financial and tax benefits for the clergy.

6. *Evaluation: Of, By, For, and To the Clergy*, by Loren B. Meade (1977), is a careful examination of the needs of both pastor and congregation in the evaluation process. Available from The Alban Institute, Suite 433 North, 4550 Montgomery Ave., Bethesda MD 20814-3341 (Tel. 800-486-1318 or 301-718-4407).

9. ENDINGS AND BEGINNINGS

1. Fortunately, some excellent resources have been developed by The Alban Institute to assist clergy during the transition time: Roy M. Oswald, *Running Through the Thistles: Terminating a Ministerial Relationship with a Parish* (publication No. AL36, 1991); *The Pastor As Newcomer* (No. AL18, 1990); and *New Beginnings: The Pastorate Start-Up Workbook* (No. AL111, 1992). The Alban Institute also offers a three-day program of training for clergy during the first 12 months in a new position. Call 800-486-1318 for information.

2. Oswald, *Running Through the Thistles*.

3. *Ritual in a New Day: An Invitation* (Nashville: Abingdon Press, 1976).

4. One that we used with our own children was *Moving*, by Fred Rogers, a First Experience Book by TV's Mister Rogers (New York: G. P. Putnam's Sons, 1987). For teenagers, there is *The Teenager's Survival Guide to Moving*, by Patricia Cooney Nida and Wendy M. Heller (New York: Atheneum, 1985).

5. From *Summary of Information for Shippers of Household Goods*, published by the Interstate Commerce Commission, Washington, D.C., p. 26. This booklet will be provided by your mover.

6. Carolyn Janik, *Positive Moves: The Complete Guide to Moving You and Your Family Across Town or Across the Nation* (New York: Grove-Atlantic, 1988). Janik covers such topics as contracting with a mover, settling into a new community, and coping with emotional stress.

7. See Oswald, *Pastor As Newcomer* and *New Beginnings*.

8. Oswald, *Pastor As Newcomer* and *New Beginnings;* see also Scott Olbert, "Who Leads Worship? Who's in the pew? How intuitive pastors can avoid worship warfare at St. Sensate's Church," *Action Information* (January/February, 1988).

11. CAREER ALTERNATIVES

1. Emily Koltnow and Lynne S. Dumas, *CONGRATULATIONS! You've Been Fired: Sound Advice for Women Who've Been Terminated, Pink-Slipped, Downsized, or Otherwise Unemployed* (New York: [Columbine] Fawcett, 1990). Although written for women in the secular marketplace, the book explores the personal and emotional issues of any person who has been fired, as well as outlining some immediate, practical steps to be taken.

2. From a resource prepared by the Northeast Career Center, 407 Nassau St., Princeton NJ 08540.

3. Christopher Chamberlin Moore, *What I REALLY Want to Do: How to Discover the Right Job* (St. Louis: CBP [Chalice] Press, 1989). See especially Part Two: "Five Steps to Career Satisfaction and Success," pp. 31-90.

4. Examples of such résumés, for various kinds of secular work, are found in a book by Yana Parker, *The Damn Good Resume Guide* (Berkeley, Calif.: Ten Speed Press, 1989).

5. Michelle Le Compte, *Job Hunter's Sourcebook: Where to Find Employment Leads and Other Job Search Resources,* 2nd ed. (Detroit: Gale Research, 1992).

6. H. Anthony Medley, *Sweaty Palms: The Neglected Art of Being Interviewed,* rev. ed. (Berkeley, Calif.: Ten Speed Press, 1992).

APPENDIX A

1. Statistics on the total number of churches, inclusive membership, and number of clergy are taken from the *Yearbook of American & Canadian Churches,* compiled by the National Council of Churches and edited by Kenneth B. Bedell (Nashville: Abingdon Press, 1994). The figures reported are for 1992, unless otherwise indicated. In the case of denominations that are the result of mergers during the past decade, membership totals are based on composite figures for the denomination prior to merger of its several component bodies, and are indicated by being listed in parentheses. The percentage of membership growth or decline is that which has occurred from 1980 to the latest year for which membership statistics are reported, if for 1990 or later. (If membership statistics predate 1990, no percentage of growth or decline is indicated.) Membership figures for 1980 are taken from a previous edition of the *Yearbook.* The percentage of denominational growth or decline, and also of clergy serving in parochial ministry, has been figured by the author on the basis of statistics reported in the *Yearbook,* and is reported to the nearest whole percentage point.

2. Salary figures are taken from the 1993 Annual Statistic Report of the 79th meeting of the Annual Church Pensions Conference. The figures listed represent a composite total of the following:

■ Cash stipend
■ Value of housing, if supplied, or cash housing allowance
■ Utilities and/or furnishings allowance
■ Social Security offset
■ Tax-sheltered annuity, if supplied
■ Children's tuition allowance, if supplied

3. Placement method classifications are taken from *Too Many Pastors?: The Clergy Job Market,* by Jackson W. Carroll and Robert L. Wilson (New York: The Pilgrim Press, 1980). Classifications indicate the degree of autonomy exercised by the pastor and by the local church in effectuating placement decisions.

Index

A

Alternative careers, 18, 142
African American, 133-35
American Baptist Church, 66
Appointive positions, 131, 135

B

Bivocational, 34
Bolles, 16, 31, 67, 106
Buddy System, 26, 71
Buyer's Remorse, 117

C

Candidating, 18, 56
Career advancement, 22
Career development centers, 15, 19, 27, 31
"Casing" a church, 74
Checklist, 19, 29, 99
Christian Church (Disciples of Christ), 62
Chronological résumé, 48, 50
Church personality, 84
Church of God, Cleveland, Tenn., 62
Church of the Nazarene, 62
Church size, 36-37
Church staff, 85
Churches, 44
Cinderella Complex, 15
Clergy couples, 129-30, 137

READER RESPONSE

TO: CLERGY PARACHUTE
The Reverend Christopher C. Moore
The Church of the Holy Comforter, Episcopal
Burmount Rd. and Bond Ave.
Drexel Hill PA 19026

❏   The section(s) of this book I have found most useful:

_____

_____

_____

❏   The part of the book I found perhaps less helpful was the section on: _____

_____

_____

The reason was: _____

_____

_____

❏   In future editions, more attention needs to be paid to:

_____

_____

_____

READER RESPONSE

My thoughts on this issue are: (Please attach an additional
sheet, if necessary.) _____

_____

_____

❏ The information on page _____ is incorrect or out of date.
The correct information is: (Please note the correct infor-
mation below, or attach an additional sheet, if necessary.)
My denomination is _____

_____

_____

_____

_____

_____

❏ I have not been able to find the following resource, listed on
page _____ of your book.

_____

_____

_____

❏ An additional resource that you should be aware of is:
(Please attach an additional sheet, if necessary.)

_____

READER RESPONSE

_____

_____

Name: _____

Address: _____

_____

_____

Printed in the United States
58687LVS00004B/32